CW00419496

AMIGURUMI

Crochet patterns for beginners

Funny & Cute Amigurumi Projects with
Easy to Follow Stitch-By-Stitch
Instructions & Clear Illustrations

Michelle Pfizer

© Copyright 2022 - All rights reserved.

The content contained within this book may not be reproduced, duplicated or transmitted without direct written permission from the author or the publisher. Under no circumstances will any blame or legal responsibility be held against the publisher, or author, for any damages, reparation, or monetary loss due to the information contained within this book. Either directly or indirectly.

Legal Notice:

This book is copyright protected. This book is only for personal use. You cannot amend, distribute, sell, use, quote or paraphrase any part, or the content within this book, without the consent of the author or publisher.

Disclaimer Notice:

Please note the information contained within this document is for educational and entertainment purposes only. All effort has been executed to present accurate, up to date, and reliable, complete information. No warranties of any kind are declared or implied. Readers acknowledge that the author is not engaging in the rendering of legal, financial, medical or professional advice. The content within this book has been derived from various sources. Please consult a licensed professional before attempting any techniques outlined in this book.

By reading this document, the reader agrees that under no circumstances is the author responsible for any losses, direct or indirect, which are incurred as a result of the use of information contained within this document, including, but not limited to, errors, omissions, or inaccuracies.

Amigurumi is a form of Japanese art dating back many years. The term Amigurumi means "a crocheted or knitted soft toy." Using thread and needles to create intricate and cute toys has been a decades-old tradition in Japan. Amigurumi has now journeyed around the globe and is enjoyed by crocheters interested in creating unique stuffed toys.

Using yarn or thread and basic crochet stitches makes it easy to create animals, dolls, fantasy creatures, etc. This gives the finished product a smooth look without any of the filling showing through wide holes.

The finished product can be large or small, depending on the yarn used. The crochet hooks generally used for Amigurumi include sizes up to 3.5mm. You will need additional supplies: embroidery needles to sew up your finished piece, polyfill to stuff your toy, and safety eyes/googly eyes as accessories.

Amigurumi crocheted toys are cute to look at and perfect for kids. Their charming button eyes, blushed cheeks, and beautiful smiles, bring immense pleasure to young children. They make an ideal gift for the holidays or birthdays, for both your kids or grandkids. They are beautiful sentimental keepsakes.

Begin with the basics and spin some magic into your creations. Start a tradition with your kids and grandkids and see how love manifests as handmade gifts surpass all the anonymity of store-bought ones.

If you are new to crocheting, don't worry! This book has been prepared for amigurumi beginners and crocheters of all levels. So, if you want to start with some simple patterns, this book is perfect for you.

Crochet Amigurumi presents a collection of 37 carefully selected animal patterns just for you. We're sure you'll find their colorful designs and clear instructions exciting and delightful to create. This book is perfect for those who love to crochet and DIY, and the patterns are simple for beginners to follow.

You will be shown and taught the basics of crochet stitches to help you get started. The abbreviations used in the book are explained on the Basic Instructions page. This will make reading the individual patterns much more effortless.

Once you've mastered the basic crochet stitches, it's relatively simple to progress to amigurumi methods. Then all you need to do is learn how to work in circles and make individual parts that will connect to build toys. The book also offers seasoned crocheters a chance to work on great patterns. So, you can use your knowledge of crochet and then accessorize your toys to make them unique.

We have named each animal as we love to make the experience personal. However, you can choose to name your toys a name that makes each of these cuties much more personal.

You can choose from seven sea creatures. Pick whichever tickles your fancy, from a dazzling starfish to a silly clownfish. Then, we move on to our home buddies, in other words, our gorgeous pets. Again, these patterns are simple, to begin with, so, Noodle the Chick and Basil the Mouse are quick to crochet.

Step into the farm, and you will find four animals to crochet. Shaun the Sheep and Penny the Pig are there waiting for you.

Once you have crocheted these animals, you can move on to our wild collection. We have a whole range of wild animals for you to choose from.

Create a hippo, elephant, bear, lion, tiger, and a baby dinosaur. You see, we haven't left any behind! Your kids will be thrilled with the wide range of animals that you can create with ease for them.

Crocheting and other yarn crafts are fun to entertain, especially when making something for a loved one. There are other great benefits of handicrafts, such as using them as a way to relieve anxiety and depression.

It has been scientifically proven that crocheting patterns release serotonin, a natural antidepressant, in the brain.

Recently, CNN reported that "in one study of more than 3,500 knitters, published in The British Journal of Occupational Therapy, 81% of [the] respondents with depression reported feeling happy after knitting. More than half reported feeling "very happy." (CNN).

Any form of craft that keeps your hands busy and your mind focused reduces excessive thinking and anxiety. It transfers the mind to a serene space due to the work's repetitive nature, for example, stitching designs and counting stitches.

Knitting and crocheting have also been proven to be very helpful for those who suffer from obsessive-compulsive disorders and those who suffer from eating disorders.

One study by the American Counselling Association showed that nearly ¾ of women with anorexia found knitting to be calming and anxiety-reducing. (Polino).

A primary cause detrimental to our health is stress. It is widely known that reducing stress decreases our chances of suffering from various diseases.

Anxiety symptoms include migraines, exhaustion, memory loss, and even heart failure. Finding time in our day for knitting or crocheting as meditation will lessen the effects of stress in our lives.

Handicraft project makes a person feel productive and, hence, builds self-esteem. When you knit, you tend to learn new skills and feel ambitious as you busy yourself with valuable means to give to others and beautifully express yourself.

Creating a handcraft will boost your confidence by simply using your imagination and focus.

Crochet amigurumi is especially beneficial for the elderly, for it has been proven to reduce dementia which can creep up on us as we grow older.

Yonas Geda, MD, a neuropsychiatrist and researcher at the Mayo Clinic, finalized a study that revealed that knitting is neuroprotective and can lessen dementia by as much as 50%. (Polino)

As you concentrate on a soft, simple, repetitively patterned crochet or knit project, you will find that your body and mind are soothed.

You will also find that even if you suffer from insomnia, knitting and working yarn crafts can rescue you from disrupted sleep patterns. Herbert Benson of the Mind/Body Medical Institute conducted a study that showed that all insomnia patients testified that their sleep had improved, with 90% being able to let go of medication while being in a program that consisted of... knitting (Caiola).

How to Do a Slip Knot

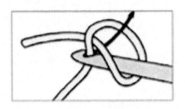
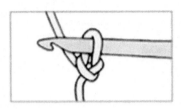

To begin, make a loop with the yarn. Hook the free end of the loop with the crochet hook through the center of the loop. Pull this through and up onto the crochet hook's working area. To tighten the loop, pull the free yarn end. The crochet hook's loop should be firm. Now you have created a slip knot.

How to Create a Slip Stitch (sl st)

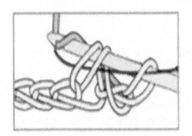
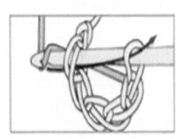

Slip stitch is used to join work in rounds or to move across a row without adding any height.

To do a row of slip stitches, turn your work and chain 1. This is not a turning chain and so you will work on the first stitch as well. Put the crochet hook in the first stitch and pull the yarn over.

Draw the yarn through both the loops of the stitch and on the hook. One slip stitch has been completed. Continue to slip stitch in each of the remaining stitches.

How to Do a Chain Stitch (ch)

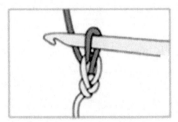

After creating the slip knot, bring the yarn over the crochet hook from back to front and hook it. Draw the hooked yarn through the loop of the slip knot on the hook and up the working area of the crochet hook. One chain stitch created.

Grip the base of the slip knot and bring the yarn from back to front over the crochet hook. Draw through the loop on the hook after hooking it. Another chain stitch created.

Repeat this step to create additional chains.

How to Do a Single Crochet (sc)

Make a chain of six. Insert the crochet hook in the second chain through the middle and under the back bar, skipping the first chain. From back to front, bring the yarn over the hook.

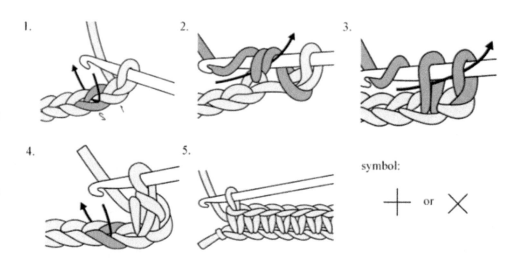

Draw the yarn up and through the chain onto the crochet hook's working region. There are two loops on the hook. From back to front, pull the yarn through the loops on the crochet hook. On the hook, one loop remains. A single crochet stitch has been made.

The hook should be inserted into the next chain. Draw the yarn through the chain stitch by hooking it from back to front. Take the yarn over again and draw through both loops. Repeat this step in each of the next chains.

One completed row of single crochet is created. To work the next row of single crochet, turn your work so that you are working on the back.

Do a chain 1, which is called the turning chain. Now insert the hook in the last stitch of the preceding row under the top two loops.

Draw yarn through the stitch and up the working region of the crochet hook by bringing it all over the hook from back to front.

On the hook, you have two loops. Pull the yarn over the loops on the crochet hook by bringing it over the hook. To finish, work a single crochet in each sc.

How to Do a Half Double Crochet (hdc)

Figure 1

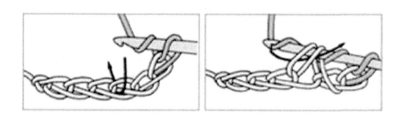

Figure 2

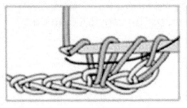 

Make a chain of 15.

From back to front, wrap the yarn around the crochet hook. The hook should be inserted in the third chain from the hook after skipping the first two chains.

Draw the yarn over the crochet hook, through the chain stitch, and up onto the hook's working region. On the hook, there are three loops. Pull the yarn over all three loops on the crochet hook by bringing it over the hook. You have completed one half-double crochet. Continue to work a half double crochet in each remaining chain.

To work the next row of half double crochet, turn your work so that you are working on the back.

Do a chain 2, which is called your turning chain. This turning chain is now your first half double crochet of the next row.

So, start working in the second stitch onwards. Continue to do half-double crochet in each remaining stitch across. Count your stitches so that you have the right number of half double crochets in each row.

How to Do a Double Crochet (dc)

Figure 1

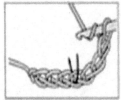 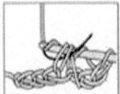 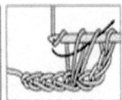

Figure 2

 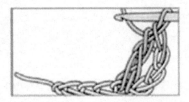

Make a chain of 15.

From back to front, bring the yarn over the hook, skip the first three chains, and then put the hook in the fourth chain.

Draw the yarn from back to front over the crochet hook, through the chain stitch, and up to the hook's working area.

On the hook, you have three loops. Take the yarn over the back of the crochet hook and bring it through the 1st two loops.

Over the hook, you will have two loops. Bring the yarn around the back of the crochet hook and drag it through both loops on the hook. One completed double crochet.

Continue to double crochet in each of the remaining chains.

To work the next row of double crochet, turn your work so that you are working on the back.

Do a chain 3, which is called your turning chain. This turning chain is now your first double crochet of the next row.

So, start working in the second stitch onwards. Continue to do a double crochet in each remaining stitch across. Count your stitches so that you have the right number of double crochets in each row.

How to Do a Backward Single Crochet (rsc)

This step is very much like a regular single crochet, except that it's done backwards.

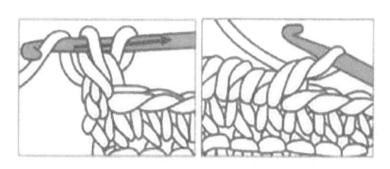

To do this, start by inserting the hook from front to back in the next stitch to the right. Then, pull the yarn over and draw it through the stitch. Bring the yarn over and draw it through the two loops on the hook.

How to Do a Treble Crochet (tc)

Make a chain of 15.

Wrap the yarn twice around the crochet hook from back to front, skip the first four chains, and put the hook into the hook's fifth chain.

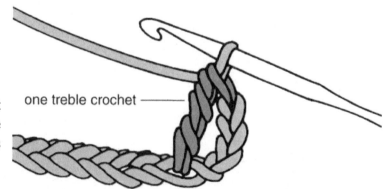

one treble crochet

Draw the yarn from back to front over the crochet hook, through the chain stitch, and onto the hook's working region.

On the hook, there are four loops.

Draw the yarn over the first two loops on the hook using the crochet hook. On the hook, you have three loops.

Bring the yarn back over the crochet hook and drag it through the hook's next two loops. On the hook, you have two loops. Put the yarn through the crochet hook and through the hook's last two

14

loops. You've just finished a treble crochet. Continue to treble crochet in each of the remaining chains.

To work the next row of treble crochet, turn your work so that you are working on the back.

Do a chain 4, which is called your turning chain. This turning chain is now your first treble crochet of the next row.

So, start working in the second stitch onwards. Continue to do a treble crochet in each remaining stitch across. Count your stitches so that you have the right number of treble crochets in each row.

Ten Steps to Do the Magic Ring (MR)

The Magic Ring is also called the Magic Circle and is used mainly in amigurumi projects. You continue to work in rounds to achieve a hollow structure that can be stuffed.

Begin by forming a circle with your yarn. Pinch and hold the yarn together where they cross. Put hook and pull yarn through your ring. Pull the loop all the way through, and up to the top of the ring.

Chain 1 and do as many single crochets as required by the pattern. Pull the yarn end and seal the circle.

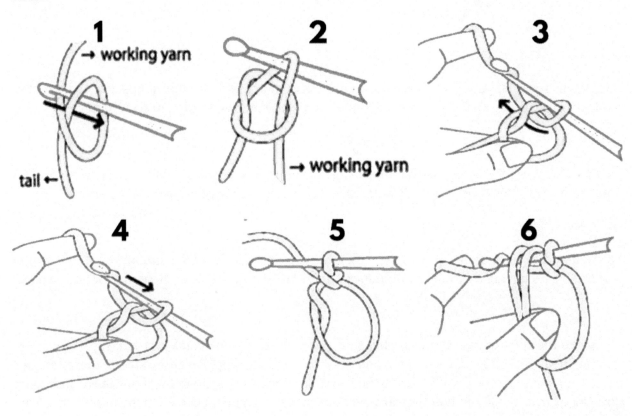

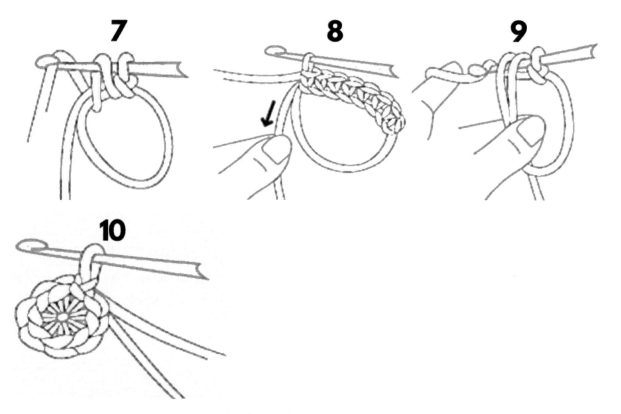

Working in Back Loop Only (BLO)

You can also crochet only in the back loop of a stitch as opposed to both the loops. Put your crochet hook underneath the back loop only and make a crochet stitch according to your pattern.

Working in Front Loop Only (FLO)

You can also crochet only in the front loop of a stitch as opposed to both the loops. Put your crochet hook underneath the front loop only and make a crochet stitch according to your pattern.

Increase (inc)

You can add to the number of stitches in a row by repeating the same stitch according to your pattern. So, an inc 1 in a row of sc would mean doing two single crochet stitches in the same space.

Decrease (dec)

To reduce the stitches in a single crochet row, you can use the sc decrease stitch. Insert the hook into the first stitch, bring the yarn over and draw through the loop. Do not complete the stitch, but put the hook into the next stitch. Bring the yarn over and draw through the loop. There should be three loops over the hook. Pull the yarn over and draw through all three loops on the hook. This creates a single crochet in the place of two single crochets of the preceding row.

What You Need for Amigurumi

1. <u>Yarn</u>: You can use any kind of yarn for amigurumi and that's what makes it easy for most crocheters. You will find three kinds of yarn to be most popular, though. They include:

- ✓ **100% cotton:** This is perfect for people who may be allergic to wool. It also gives a good surface finish to the product.

- ✓ **Blended yarn:** This is a lightweight yarn that is perfect for large projects.

- ✓ **Acrylic yarn:** This is the most economical yarn to work with. It is a fibrous yarn, so your stitches need to be tight to keep the product in shape.

2. <u>Crochet Hook</u>: Amigurumi projects require the crochet hook to be of a smaller gauge so that the stuffing does not show through. Each pattern will provide you with information about the exact hook size to use. Ideally, the crochet hook size should match with the yarn used.

3. <u>Stuffing</u>: Polyfill stuffing is easily available online and is used to stuff the parts of your toy.

4. <u>Safety eyes/ Beads/ Googly eyes</u>: To accentuate your toy, you can use safety eyes in various sizes. For toys that will be played with by smaller children, it is advisable to sew beads on the toys so they cannot come off easily. Googly eyes are another option that can be glued to the toy. Safety precautions need to be taken in all these cases.

5. <u>Pipe cleaners/Wire</u>: You may need these to give your toy structure and movability.

6. <u>Scissors</u>: Make sure it is a good, sharp pair of scissors to make clean cuts in the yarn.

7. <u>Dog slicker brush</u>: This item is optional, but it is often used to make fuzzy amigurumi. It can be used to brush the amigurumi to agitate the fibers to create that brushed fur look!

8. <u>Felt</u>: Felt is usually cut in oval shapes and used for the noses, as well as for the lining of ears, hands, and feet. The colors used most often are white, brown, beige, and black.

Abbreviations Used in the Book:

- ✓ R–row
- ✓ st – stitch
- ✓ ch – chain
- ✓ sl st– slip stitch
- ✓ sc – single crochet
- ✓ hdc – half double crochet

- ✓ dc – double crochet
- ✓ tr – treble crochet
- ✓ dec – decrease
- ✓ inc – increase
- ✓ BLO – in back loops only
- ✓ FO – fasten off

- ✓ MR – Magic Ring
- ✓ CC – change color
- ✓ () – repeat instructions

NOTE: Unless otherwise stated, the items are worked in rounds, with each row finishing with a **sl st** to the up of the first **st**.

Glossary & Common Terms

Terms & Common Measurements

Term	Description		Measurement	Description
*	repeat the instructions following the single asterisk as directed		" or in	inch
* *	repeat instructions between asterisks as many times as directed or repeat at specified		cm	centimeter
{ }	work instructions within brackets as many times as directed		g	gram
[ ]	work instructions within brackets as many times as directed		m	meter
( )	work instructions within parentheses as many times as directed or work a group of		mm	millimeter
			oz	ounce
			yd	yard

Abbreviation	Description		Abbreviation	Description
alt	alternate		FPtr	front post treble crochet
approx	approximately		hdc	half double crochet
beg	begin/beginning		hdc2tog	half double crochet 2 stitches together
bet	between		inc	increase
BL or BLO	back loop or back loop only		lp	loop
bo	bobble		m	marker
BP	back post		MC	main color
BPdc	back post double crochet		pat or patt	pattern
BPdtr	back post double treble crochet		pc	popcorn stitch
BPhdc	back post half double crochet		pm	place marker
BPsc	back post single crochet		prev	previous
BPtr	back post treble crochet		ps or puff	puff stitch
CC	contrasting color		rem	remaining
ch	chain stitch		rep	repeat
ch-	refer to chain or space previously made, e.g., ch-1 space		rnd	round
ch-sp	chain space		RS	right side
CL	cluster		sc	single crochet
cont	continue		sc2tog	single crochet 2 stitches together
dc	double crochet		sh	shell
dc2tog	double crochet 2 stitches together		sk	skip
dec	decrease		sl st	slip stitch
dtr	double treble crochet		sm or sl m	slip marker
edc	extended double crochet		sp	space
ehdc	extended half double crochet		st	stitch
esc	extended single crochet		tbl	through back loop
etr	extended treble crochet		tch or t-ch	turning chain
FL or FLO	front loop or front loop only		tog	together
foll	following		tr	treble crochet
FP	front post		tr2tog	treble crochet 2 stitches together
FPdc	front post double crochet		trtr	triple treble crochet
FPdtr	front post double treble crochet		WS	wrong side
FPhdc	front post half double crochet		yo	yarn over
FPsc	front post single crochet		yoh	yarn over hook

Abbreviation & Term Differences between the U.S., United Kingdom (U.K.) and Canada.

U.S./Canada 🇺🇸 🇨🇦	U.K. 🇬🇧
slip stitch (sl st)	slip stitch (ss)
single crochet (sc)	double crochet (dc)
half double crochet (hdc)	half treble (htr)
double crochet (dc)	treble (tr)
treble (tr)	double treble (dtr)
double treble (dtr)	triple treble (trtr)
U.S. 🇺🇸	**U.K./Canada** 🇬🇧 🇨🇦
gauge	tension
yarn over (yo)	yarn over hook (yoh)

Y ou need to practice the basic stitches and master the different crochet terminologies to create your masterpiece.

Although you can always look with this book for a quick reference on the stitch you must use, it is more comfortable to crochet if you've memorized how to do a certain stitch.

You will also encounter some of the crochet terms in their abbreviated form so you can practice your crochet language.

Picot Stitch

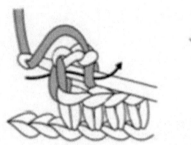 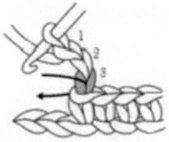

Some patterns use "**p**" to symbolize a picot stitch. Picots are used to add decoration to a pattern and sometimes as fillers.

On the area where you're planning to add a picot stitch, do 3 chain stitches.

Put your hook into the 3rd chain from your loop.

Make a sl st to close the stitch.

Add the picot stitches to the areas where you need to put them.

Cluster Stitch

Cluster stitch has no known abbreviation, but some patterns go with "**cl**" as the cluster's abbreviation. A cluster usually forms a triangle.

To best illustrate, you will need dc stitches to make a cluster. You must leave each of the 2 remaining loops open in the first 3 dcs.

To start, yarn over and insert your hook through the next stitch. Make your first dc, but when you only have 2 remaining loops on your hook, don't slip the thread through the remaining 2 loops. Leave the loops hanging from your hook, and you'd end up with one unfinished dc.

Yarn over and put your hook into the next stitch to make your 2nd dc.

Then, you have four loops on your hook.

21

Yarn over and slip the thread through the first 2 loops of your 2nd dc. At this stage, you have three loops on your hook. Leave them hanging from your hook. You should have 2 unfinished dc stitches.

Do the same with the remaining dc stitches you need to make to create your cluster stitch.

At this stage, you should have four unfinished dc stitches.

Yarn over, then slip the thread through the 5 loops on your hook, and you will produce 1 dc cluster.

Popcorn Stitch

This stitch is named as such because it does look like one. A popcorn stitch is a rounded and compact stitch that pops out. You can place your popcorn stitch in front or back—it all depends on the effect you want to achieve in your piece.

In making a popcorn stitch, you need 5 dc together in one stitch.

Remove your hook from your current loop; make sure not to lose the current loop and just drop it in the meantime.

Insert your hook in front (as shown) of the first dc in the group if you want to pop your stitch in front. Insert your hook from the back if you want it to pop at the back.

Hook your dropped loop and let it slip through the dc stitch to get a popcorn stitch.

V-Stitches

V-stitches resemble the letter V, hence the name. You can crochet loosely using this stitch, especially if you want to create lacy designs. You can also make your stitches tight and compressed.

To begin, do a dc, ch 1, and another dc on the same stitch.

In between the 2 stitches, the single ch st separates the 2 dcs (to resemble the letter V).

Keep in mind that the 2 dcs should be on the same stitch.

Shell Stitch

The shell stitch is an adaptable crochet stitch and comes in different variations.

To begin, do dc 4 on the same stitch.

You should be able to come up with an inverted cluster.

A shell stitch is easier to do than a cluster stitch.

You can close each dc immediately, and you don't need to wait for the last dc to close the stitch.

Puff Stitch

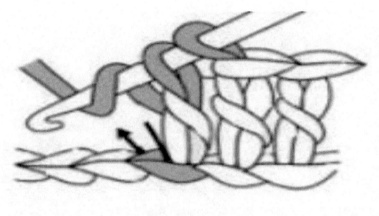

The puff stitches create a different texture to your work. This stitch follows the same procedure as the cluster, but you need to place all the dc stitches in the same stitch. You also need to work on 3 dc stitches to create one puff stitch.

To start, make a dc stitch and leave the last 2 loops open or hanging. You should have 1 unfinished dc stitch on your hook.

Start with your 2nd dc stitch on the same stitch as the first unfinished dc. Leave the 3 loops hanging from your hook.

Now, begin your 3rd and last dc for your puff stitch and bring it together with the first 2 dc stitches on the same spot. Yarn over, then slip the thread through the first 2 loops, and you will have 4 loops hanging on your hook. Yarn over, then slip the thread through the 4 remaining loops, and you will get a dc puff stitch.

Tapestry Crochet

Tapestry in the round is the most common way to work tapestry crochet.

This example uses single crochet.

Start with a round of stitches.

Hold the new yarn color behind your work and simply crochet over this new color a few stitches to secure it.

Stitch before where you want to use your new color, insert into the upcoming stitch, but yarn over with the new color, and pull through as normal.

The new color stitch work as your normal stitch, but this time you work over the yarn tail from the original color.

Repeat this same process when you want to switch back to the original color.

Stitch before you want to use your original color, insert into the upcoming stitch, but yarn over with the original color, and pull through as normal.

The original color stitch works like your normal stitch, but this time works over the yarn tail from the new color.

Surface Slip Stitch

Start with a field of crochet stitches; this example is single crochet.

Insert your hook from top to bottom through the work you'd like to start the surface crochet stitches.

From the bottom, take the yarn for the surface crochet, make a loop over the crochet hook, and gently pull through the work.

Pull through a loop from the yarn's working end, and then pull through the work like a slip stitch through the other loop.

Continue in the desired pattern.

Working in Rows

In short, this simply means working back and forth from one side to the other.

You will want to rely on your pattern here because it will tell you how many to chain. For this example, we will use a single crochet. Let's say your pattern asked you to chain 10:

You will then single crochet in the first chain from the hook and all the following chains.

Now turn your work and chain 1.

Now single crochet in all stitches, starting with the 2nd stitch from the hook; unless directed otherwise by the pattern.

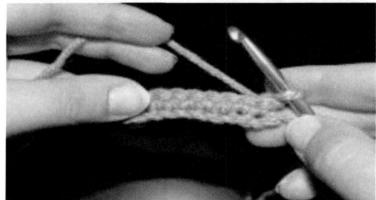

Working in Rounds

In short, it simply means that you will be working in a circle.

You will want to rely on your pattern here because it will tell you how many to chain.

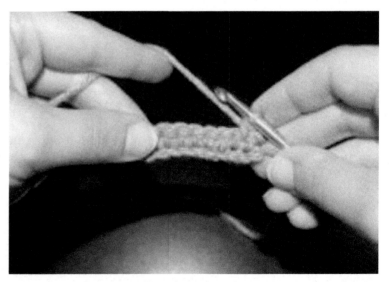

Chain the required number of chains.

Connect the first and last stitch with a slip stitch. This will form a ring.

In the first round, you will crochet into each stitch unless directed by the pattern.

Slip stitches the last stitch and the first stitch together to finish up each round.

To start your next round chain (we are chaining one for single crochet) and chain all the way around. Finish with a slip stitch to connect.

Insert the crochet hook into the upcoming stitch and then yarn over.

Gently pull the yarn through only 1 loop on the crochet hook. Now release the loose end of the original color of yarn and hold the new color yarn against the piece of work.

Yarn over the crochet hook with the new color of yarn that you have selected.

Gently pull the new color of yarn through the remaining 2 loops left on the crochet hook.

Now, with the new color of yarn, continue your pattern as directed.

Amigurumi Patterns

Now let's crochet some of our much-loved pets! These furry pals are perfect animals to crochet, especially for kids.

With cute faces, they represent the love that pets have for us. Create them in vibrant colors and see your child's face light up in awe. Let's make all of them now!

1. Noodle the Chick

Let Noodle, the Chick, dazzle you with his sparkling eyes. This little chick is perfect for Easter, also, as a holiday gift. With simple stitches, you can ruffle up Noodle in no time. Make him in different colors to attract your little ones.

What You Need:

- ➢ DK/ worsted yarn in the color of your choice
- ➢ Orange yarn
- ➢ 4 mm crochet hook
- ➢ A pair of 6 mm safety eyes
- ➢ Stuffing
- ➢ Embroidery needle to sew

Body:

1. R1: 6 sc in MR (6)
2. R2: inc in each st (12)
3. R3: (sc 1, inc 1) * 6 (18)
4. R4: (sc 5, inc 1) * 3 (21)
5. R5: (sc 6, inc 1) * 3 (24)
6. R6: (sc 7, inc 1) * 3 (27)
7. R7: (sc 8, inc 1) * 3 (30)
8. R8: (sc 9, inc 1) * 3 (33)
9. R9: (sc 10, inc 1) *3 (36)
10. R10–17: sc in each st (36)
11. Stuff the body.
12. Attach eyes at R10.
13. R18: (sc 4, dec 1) * 6 (30)
14. R19: (sc 3, dec 1) *6 (24)
15. R20: (sc 2, dec 1) *6 (18)
16. R21: (sc 1, dec 1) *6 (12)
17. R22: dec 1 * 6 (6)
18. Fasten off and weave in the ends.
19. Cut four pieces of yarn about 2 inches long and attach them to the top of the head with a knot. Trim the length accordingly.

Wings (Make 2):

1. R1: 5 sc in MR (5)
2. R2: Ch1, turn, sc in 1st sc, 2 hdc, 3 dc, 2 hdc, slst
3. R3: Ch1, turn, sc, sc, sc, inc 1, inc 1, inc 1, sc, sc, sc
4. FO leaving a long tail to sew.
5. Sew the head of the wings on the side of the body at R11.

Beak:

1. Use orange yarn to embroider straight stitches around R12 and R13 between the eyes.

Feet:

1. Use orange yarn.
2. [Ch5, sl st in 2nd ch through the hook, (ch2, sl st in each of these 2ch) *2, sl st in remaining 3 ch] * 2
3. FO leaving a long tail to sew.
4. Sew the feet to the under part of the body towards the front.

2. Basil the Mouse

A mouse around the house can be fun, too. Let those adoring eyes draw you towards him. Basil is super quick to create and can be made in a variety of colors. Change the crochet hook size to create larger versions of him.

What You Need:

- ➢ DK/ worsted yarn in the color of your choice
- ➢ Pink yarn
- ➢ 3 mm and 3.5 mm crochet hook
- ➢ A pair of 4 mm safety eyes
- ➢ Stuffing
- ➢ Embroidery needle to sew

Body:

1. Use 3.5 mm hook
2. R1: Ch2, four sc in 2nd ch from hook (4)
3. R2: (inc 1, sc 1) *2 (6)
4. R3: (sc 1, inc 1) *3 (9)
5. R4: (sc 2, inc 1) *3 (12)
6. R5: sc in each st (12)
7. R6: (sc 2, inc 1) *4 (16)
8. R7: (sc 3, inc 1) *4 (20)
9. Attach eyes at R4 with 5 stitches in between.
10. R8–13: sc in each st (20)
11. R14: (sc 3, dec 1) * 4 (16
12. Stuff the body.
13. R15: (sc 2, dec 1) * 4 (12)
14. R16: dec in each st (6)
15. R17: (skip next st, sl st) * 3 (3)
16. R18: Ch 20
17. Fasten off and weave in the ends

Ears (Make 2):

1. Use 3 mm hook
2. R1: 6 sc in MR (6)
3. R2: inc in each st (12)
4. FO leaving a long tail to sew.
5. Sew the ears at R10.
6. Using pink yarn, embroider around R1 of the body to look like a nose.

3. Peanut the Dog

Now, who doesn't want their favorite pet as a toy? For those who cannot keep the real ones at home, this is the best option. So, make this cuddly dog and have fun playing with him for years. With his cute tongue sticking out, he will be a great companion all day long.

What You Need:

- ➢ DK/ worsted yarn in the color of your choice
- ➢ Red yarn
- ➢ 3.5 mm crochet hook
- ➢ A pair of 4 mm safety eyes
- ➢ Stuffing
- ➢ Embroidery needle to sew

Head:

1. R1: 6 sc in MR (6)
2. R2: inc in each st (12)
3. R3: (sc 1, inc 1) * 6 (18)
4. R4: (sc 2, inc 1) * 6 (24)
5. R5–9: sc in each st (24)
6. R10: (sc 3, inc 1) * 6 (30)
7. R11: (sc 4, inc 1) * 6 (36)
8. R12: (sc 5, inc 1) * 5, sc 6 (41)
9. R13: (sc 6, inc 1) * 5, sc 6 (46)
10. R14: (sc 7, inc 1) * 5, sc 6 (51)
11. R15–17: sc in each st (51)
12. R18: (sc 7, dec 1) * 5, sc 6 (46)
13. R19: (sc 6, dec 1) * 5, sc 6 (41)
14. R20: (sc 5, dec 1) * 5, sc 6 (36)
15. R21: sc in each st (36)
16. R22: (sc 4, dec 1) *6 (30)
17. R23: (sc 3, dec 1) *6 (24)
18. R24: (sc 2, dec 1) *6 (18)

19. Attach safety eyes in place. Stuff the head.
20. R25: (sc 1, dec 1) * 6 (12)
21. R26: dec * 6 (6)
22. Fasten off and weave in the ends.
23. Using black yarn, sew a nose with straight stitches.

Ears (Make 2):

1. R1: 3 sc in MR (3)
2. R2: inc in each st (6)
3. R3: (sc 1, inc 1) * 3 (9)
4. R4: sc in each st (9)
5. R5: (sc 2, inc 1) * 3 (12)
6. R6: sc in each st (12)
7. R7: (sc 3, inc 1) * 3 (15)
8. R8: sc in each st (15)
9. R9: (sc 4, inc 1) * 3 (18)
10. R10–16: sc in each st (18)
11. Sew the open ends using sc. FO leaving a long tail to sew. Sew the ears to the head's side.

Body:

1. R1: 8 sc in MR (8)
2. R2: inc in each st (16)
3. R3: (sc 1, inc 1) * 8 (24)
4. R4: (sc 2, inc 1) * 8 (32)
5. R5: (sc 3, inc 1) * 8 (40)
6. R6–17: sc in each st (40)
7. R18: (sc 3, dec 1) *8 (32)
8. R19–25: sc in each st (32)
9. R26: (sc 2, dec 1) * 8 (24)
10. R27: (sc 1, dec 1) * 8 (16)
11. Stuff the body.
12. R28: dec * 8 (8)
13. FO leaving a long tail to sew.
14. Attach the head to the body.

Legs (Make 4):

1. R1: 6 sc in MR (6)
2. R2: inc in each st (12)
3. R3: (sc 1, inc 1) * 6 (18)
4. R4: (sc 2, inc 1) * 6 (24)
5. R5–6: sc in each st (24)
6. R7: sc 12, (sc 2, dec 1) * 3 (21)
7. R8: sc 12, (sc 1, dec 1) * 3 (18)
8. R9: sc 12, (dec 1) * 3 (15)
9. R10–21: sc in each st (15)
10. Stuff the legs and FO, leaving a long tail to sew.
11. Sew the legs closed and sew in place on the body.

Tail:

1. Ch 10, sc in 2nd ch through the hook, sc, sc, hdc in 6 sts.
2. FO and sew the tail to the body.

Tongue:

1. Use red yarn
2. R1: Ch 4, sc in 2nd ch through hook, sc, sc R2: Ch1, turn, inc 1, sc, inc 1
3. R3: Ch1, turn, sc in each st
4. R4: Ch1, turn, dec 1, sc, dec 1
5. FO and sew to the muffle.

4. Bucky the Bunny

Bucky is such an adorable little bunny that you would love to keep around the house. With perfect long ears, he is a unique gift for everyone. You can make Bucky colorful, too. Just run wild with your imagination and you could have a whole family of bunnies ready to play with.

What You Need:

➤ DK/ worsted yarn in the color of your choice
➤ 4 mm crochet hook
➤ A pair of 6 mm safety eyes
➤ Stuffing
➤ Embroidery needle to sew

Head & Body:

1. R1: 6 sc in MR (6)
2. R2: inc in each st (12)
3. R3: (sc 1, inc 1) *6 (18)
4. R4: (sc 2, inc 1) *6 (24)
5. R5: (sc 3, inc 1) *6 (30)
6. R6: (sc 4, inc 1) *6 (36)
7. R7: (sc 5, inc 1) *6 (42)
8. R8–14: sc in each st (42)
9. Attach safety eyes at R11.
10. R15: (sc 5, dec 1) *6 (36)
11. R16: (sc 4, dec 1) *6 (30)
12. R17: (sc 3, dec 1) *6 (24)
13. R18: (sc 2, dec 1) *6 (18)
14. R19: (sc 1, dec 1) * 6 (12)
15. Stuff the head and continue working the body.
16. R20: (sc 5, inc 1) * 2 (14)
17. R21: (sc 1, inc 1) * 7 (21)
18. R22: (sc 2, inc 1) * 7 (28)
19. R23–28: sc in each st (28)
20. R29: (sc 2, dec 1) *7 (21)
21. R30: (sc 1, dec 1) *7 (14)
22. R31: dec * 7 (7)
23. Stuff the body well.
24. Fasten off and weave in the ends.

Ears (Make 2):

1. R1: 5 sc in MR (5)
2. R2: inc in each st (10)
3. R3: (sc 1, inc 1) * 5 (15)
4. R4–5: sc in each st (15)
5. R6: (sc 3, dec 1) * 3 (12)
6. R7: sc in each st (12)
7. R8: (sc 2, dec 1) * 3 (9)
8. R9: sc in each st (9)
9. R10: (sc 1, dec 1) *3 (6)
10. FO leaving a long tail to sew.
11. Sew the ears to the up of the head.

Arms (Make 2):

1. R1: 6 sc in MR (6)
2. R2: (sc 1, inc 1) * 3 (9)
3. R3: sc in each st (9)
4. R4: (sc 1, dec 1) * 3 (6)
5. R5–8: sc in each st
6. FO leaving a long tail to sew.

7. Tie the arms to the face of the body.

Legs (Make 2):

1. R1: 6 sc in MR (6)
2. R2: inc in each st (12)
3. R3: (sc 1, inc 1) *6 (18)
4. R4-6: sc in each st (18)
5. Stuff the legs.
6. R7: (sc 1, dec 1) * 6 (12)
7. R8: dec * 6 (6)
8. R9: sc in each st (6)
9. FO leaving a long tail to sew. Attach the legs to the body.

Tail:

1. R1: 6 sc in MR (6)
2. R2: inc in each st (12)
3. R3: sc in each st (12)
4. R4: dec * 6 (6)
5. FO leaving a long tail to sew. Attach the tail to the body.

5. Mia the Pusheen Cat

This cartoon cat character is a lovable crochet toy that you can create for your kids. You can change the colors of the yarn to make her attractive. This cuddly toy is perfect for kids who love the Pusheen character. So, go ahead and have fun creating this cute furry pal..

What You Need:

➢ DK/ worsted yarn in light grey (L), dark grey (D), black (B)
➢ 4 mm crochet hook
➢ A pair of 6 mm safety eyes
➢ Stuffing

➢ Embroidery needle to sew

Body:

1. Use L
2. R1: 6 sc in MR (6)
3. R2: sc inc in each st (12)
4. R3: (sc in 1 st, sc inc 1) * 6 (18)
5. R4: (sc in 2 sts, sc inc 1) *6 (24)
6. R5: (sc in 3 sts, sc inc 1) *6 (30)
7. R6: (sc in 4 sts, sc inc 1) *6 (36)
8. R7: sc in 3 sts, CC D sc in 9 sts, CC L sc in 24 sts (36)
9. R8: sc in 3 sts, CC D sc in 10 sts, CC L sc in 23 sts (36)
10. R9-10: sc in each st (36)
11. R11: sc in 3 sts, CC D sc in 11 sts, CC L sc in 22 sts (36)
12. R12: sc in 3 sts, CC D sc in 12 sts, CC L sc in 21 sts (36)
13. R13–19: sc in each st (36)

14. Attach safety eyes.
15. R20: (sc in 4 sts, sc dec 1) * 6 (30)
16. R21: (sc in 3 sts, sc dec 1) * 6 (24)
17. R22: (sc in 2 sts, sc dec 1) * 6 (18)
18. R23: (sc in 1 st, sc dec 1) * 6 (12)
19. Stuff the head and continue working the body R24: (dec) * 6 (6)
20. Fasten off and weave in the ends.

Tail:

1. Use D
2. R1: 6 sc in MR (6)
3. R2: (sc in 1 st, sc inc 1) * 3 (9)
4. CC L
5. R3–4: sc in each st (9)
6. CC D
7. R5–6: sc in each st (9)
8. CC L
9. R7–8: sc in each st (9)
10. CC D
11. R9: sc in each st (9)
12. Stuff the tail.
13. R10: (sc in 1 sts, sc dec 1) *3 (6)

14. Tighten off leaving a long tail to sew.
15. Attach the tail to the body.

Ears (Make 2):

1. Use L
2. R1: 3 sc in MR (3)
3. R2: sc inc in each st (6)
4. R3: sc in each st (6)
5. R4: (sc in 1 st, sc inc 1) * 3 (9)
6. Tighten off leaving a long tail to sew.
7. Attach the ears to the top of the body.

Feet (Make 4):

1. Use L
2. R1: 3 sc in MR (3)
3. R2: sc inc in each st (6)
4. Tighten off leaving a long tail to sew.
5. Attach the feet to the bottom of the body.
6. Using B embroider a mouth and whiskers.
7. Sew three straight stitches above the eyes with D.

6. Buzz the Bee Bottle Cover

What You Need:

➢ In this pattern, I am using yellow, black, and white cotton yarn.
➢ Hook size N-3.00mm.
➢ Fiber
➢ Safety eyes
➢ Sewing needle
➢ Embroidery yarn
➢ Stitch marker
➢ Stitches Used in this Pattern
➢ Magic ring
➢ Single crochet stitch
➢ Slip stitch
➢ Double crochet stitch
➢ Crochet in continuous rounds and don't forget to use a stitch marker at the beginning of each round.

Head and Body:

1. With the black yarn, begin with a magic ring.
2. R1: 6 SC into the magic ring.

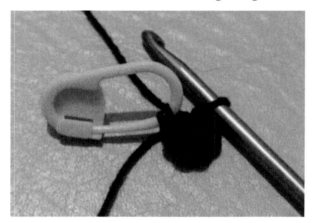

3. R2: (INC) X6 = 12 Sts.
4. R3 to R4: Sc around in all 12 St = 12 Sts.

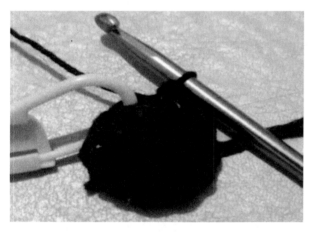

5. Change to the yellow color by slip stitch into the first stitch in the next round. Then, tie the two strings together to secure the new color but don't cut the black yarn.

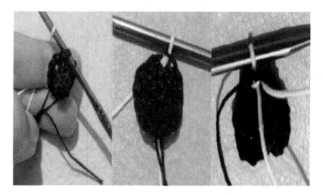

6. R5: (Sc in next St, INC in the next stitch) X6 = 18 Sts.

7. R6: (Sc in the next 2 St, INC in the next stitch) X6 = 24 Sts.

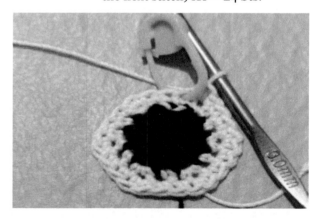

8. R7: (Sc in next 3 St, INC in the next stitch) X6 = 30 Sts.

9. R8: (Sc in next 4 St, INC in the next stitch) X6 = 36 Sts.

10. Change to the black thread.

11. R9: (Sc in next 5 St, INC in the next stitch) X6 = 42 Sts.

12. From R10 to R11: Sc around in all 42 St = 42 Sts.

13. Change to the yellow thread.
14. From Rnd 12 to Rnd 14: Sc around in all 42 St = 42 Sts

15. Before you finish the last single crochet on Rnd 14, change to the black yarn.

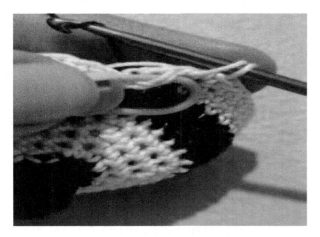

16. From Rnd 15 to Rnd 16: Sc around in all 42 St = 42 Sts.
17. R17: (Sc in next 5 St, Dec in the next stitch) X6 = 36 Sts.
18. Before you finish the last single crochet on Rnd 17, change to the yellow yarn.

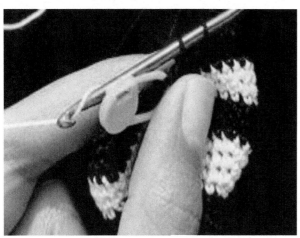

19. R18: (Sc in next 4 St, Dec in the next stitch) X6 = 30 Sts.
20. R19: (Sc in next 3 St, Dec in the next stitch) X6 = 24 Sts.
21. R20: (Sc in next 2 St, Dec in the next stitch) X6 = 18 Sts.
22. Before you finish the last single crochet on Rnd 20, change to the black yarn.

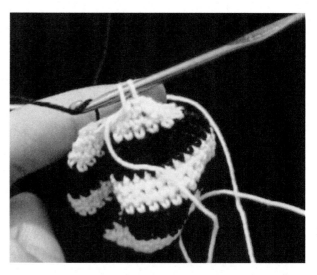

23. R21: (Sc in next St, Dec in the next stitch) X6 = 12 Sts.
24. Before you finish the last single crochet on Rnd 21, change to the yellow yarn.
25. Then, cut the black yarn and tie the tail of the black yarn with the yellow yarn to secure it.

From here, I have finished the body pattern and I will start the head pattern:

1. R22: (Sc in next St, INC in the next stitch) X6 = 18 Sts.
2. R23: (Sc in next 2 St, INC in the next stitch) X6 = 24 Sts.
3. R24: (Sc in next 3 St, INC in the next stitch) X6 = 30 Sts.
4. R25: (Sc in next 4 St, INC in the next stitch) X6 = 36 Sts.

5. R26: (Sc in next 5 St, INC in the next stitch) X6 = 42 Sts.

6. From Rnd 27 to Rnd 29: Sc around in all 42 St = 42 Sts

7. Stuff it with fiber and place the eyes on Rnd 5 at about 4 stitches apart.

8. R30: (Sc in the next 5 St, Dec in the next stitch) X6 = 36 Sts.
9. R31: (Sc in the next 4 St, Dec in the next stitch) X6 = 30 Sts.
10. R32: (Sc in the next 3 St, Dec in the next stitch) X6 = 24 Sts.
11. R33: (Sc in next 2 St, Dec in the next stitch) X6 = 18 Sts.
12. R34: (Sc in next St, Dec in the next stitch) X6 = 12 Sts.

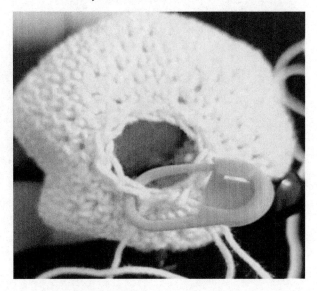

13. Stuff it with fiber.

14. Rnd 35: (Dec) X6 = 6 Sts.

15. Finish with SL St. Tighten off, leaving a tail, and use it to close the hole.
16. Pass the tail in loops in front of 6 stitches, then pull it tight and leave the end of the tail in the back to sew the bee to the cover.

Wings:

1. Make two wings with the white yarn.
2. Begin with a magic ring.
3. R1: 6 SC into the magic ring.
4. R2: (INC) X6 = 12 Sts.
5. R3: (Sc in next St, INC in the next stitch) X6 = 18 Sts.
6. From Rnd 4 to Rnd 7: Sc around in all 18 St = 18 Sts.
7. Rnd 8: (Sc in next St, Dec in the next stitch) X6 = 12 Sts.
8. From Rnd 9 to Rnd 10: Sc around in all 12 St = 12 Sts.
9. Rnd 11: (Dec) X6 = 6 Sts.
10. Rnd 12: Sc around in all 6 St = 6 Sts.
11. Finish with SL St. Tighten off leaving a tail for sewing.

Antennas:

1. Make two with the black yarn
2. Begin with a magic ring.
3. R1: 6 SC into the magic ring.
4. R2: (INC) X6 = 12 Sts.
5. R7: Sc around in all 12 St = 12 Sts.

6. R4: (Dec) X6 = 6 Sts.
7. From Rnd 5 to Rnd 8: Sc around in all 6 St = 6 Sts.
8. Finish with SL St. Tighten off leaving a tail for sewing

Assembly:

1. To be sure that you have placed everything in the right position, use pins to affix each part in its place before sewing them.
2. Sew the antenna to the sides of the head.

3. Sew the wings on the back.

4. Embroider the mouth and the eyebrows.

5. Now you have finished the bee.

7. Bottle Cover for 220 mL Baby Bottle

I will crochet the cover for a 220 ml baby bottle:

1. With the yellow yarn, begin with a magic ring.
2. R1: 6 SC into the magic ring.
3. R2: (INC) X6 = 12 Sts.

4. R3: (Sc in next St, INC in the next stitch) X6 = 18 Sts.

5. R4: (Sc in the next 2 St, INC in the next stitch) X6 = 24 Sts.

6. R5: (Sc in the next 3 St, INC in the next stitch) X6 = 30 Sts.

7.   R6: (Sc in the next 4 St, INC in the next stitch) X6 = 36 Sts.

9.   R8: (Sc in the next 6 St, INC in the next stitch) X6 = 48 Sts.

8.   R7: (Sc in the next 5 St, INC in the next stitch) X6 = 42 Sts.

10.   R9: (Sc in the next 7 St, INC in the next stitch) X6 = 54 Sts.

11. R10: (Sc in the next 8 St, INC in the next stitch) X6 = 60 Sts.

12. R11: In the back loop only, Sc around in all 60 St = 60 Sts.

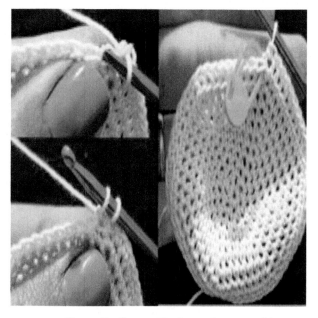

13. From Rnd 12 to Rnd 43: Sc around in all 60 St = 60 Sts.

NOTE: You can continue Sc around until you reach your desired length, but here, because I am using a 220 ml bottle, I only need 32 rnds more.

14. Before you finish the last single crochet on Rnd 43, change to the black yarn.
15. Then, cut the yellow yarn and tie the tail of the yellow yarn with the black yarn to secure it.

16. Rnd 44: Dc around in all 60 St = 60 Sts.

17. Finish with SL St. Tighten off and hide the tail in the back of your work.
18. Sew the bee to the cover.

Ready to begin your amigurumi journey with us? So let's dive into the sea.

You will absolutely love making these gorgeous sea creatures with their vibrant colors. From a turtle to a whale, we have it all.

Using easy-to-read patterns, you can whip up these beauties in no time. These huggable crochet toys are perfect as gifts or just to adorn your home.

8. Pebbles the Starfish

This cute little starfish is waiting to be played with. You can create him in any color you use. This starfish is made by joining two pieces together and stuffing the whole. Sew a smile on his face and let him brighten up your day.

What You Need:

- ➤ DK/ worsted yarn in color of your choice 50g
- ➤ Black yarn
- ➤ 3 mm and 3.5 mm crochet hook
- ➤ Stuffing
- ➤ Embroidery needle to sew

Body (Make 2):

1. Using a 3.5 mm hook
2. R1: 5 sc in MR (5)
3. R2: 2 sc in each st (10)
4. R3: (sc 1, inc 1) *5 (15)
5. R4: (sc 2, inc 1) *5 (20)
6. R5: (sc 3, inc 1) *5 (25)
7. Now change to a 3 mm hook
8. R6: (Ch 14, sl st into the 2nd ch from hook, sl st, 2 sc, 4 hdc, 4 dc, 1 tr, sl st in the next 4 sts of the body) * 5

9. R7: (1 tr in the first st on the arm, 4 dc, 4 hdc, 2 sc, 2 sl st, continue to sl st in the sts of R6 till you reach the next arm) * 5 [Figures below]
10. Do not FO.

Assembly:

1. Keeping the two pieces together, sl st around the edges while stuffing as you go.
2. Using black yarn, embroider eyes and mouth.

9. Inky the Octopus

Inky is a cute little octopus that you can complete in no time. A stuffed body and simple tentacles—this pattern couldn't have been easier. Choose any color you like and make her as bright as possible.

What You Need:

> - DK/ worsted yarn in color of your choice 50g
> - Scraps of white yarn
> - Black yarn
> - 3.5 mm crochet hook
> - A pair of 6 mm safety eyes
> - Stuffing
> - Embroidery needle to sew

Body:

1. Use yarn color of your choice
2. R1: 6 sc in MR (6)
3. R2: inc in each st (12)
4. R3: (sc1, inc 1) *6 (18)
5. R4: (sc 2, inc 1) *6 (24)
6. R5: (sc 3, inc 1) *6 (30)
7. R6: (sc 4, inc 1) *6 (36)
8. R7: (sc 5, inc 1) *6 (42)
9. R8–13: sc in each st (42)
10. R14: (sc 5, dec 1) *6 (36)
11. R15: (sc 4, dec 1) *6 (30)
12. You can now attach the eyes between R12 and R13 with 8 sts in between. Using black yarn, sew a mouth on R14.
13. R16: (sc 3, dec 1) *6 (24)
14. R17: (sc 2, dec 1) *6 (18)
15. Stuff the body.
16. R18: (sc 1, dec 1) *6 (12)
17. R19: dec in each st (6)
18. FO leaving a long tail to sew.

Tentacles (Make 8): This is made with two pieces sewn together: one in the main color and one in white.

With white yarn:

1. R1: Ch 20, turn
2. R2: sc in 2nd ch through the hook, sc in next, hdc in 17 sts FO.
3. Repeat the same with yarn in the main color but do not FO. Keep the pieces together and then sc in 18, 3 sc, sc in 18. Leave a long tail to sew

Assembly:

1. Sew the tentacles on the head around R5.

10.   Jell-O the Jellyfish

A variation of the octopus' pattern, this jellyfish will be another cool addition to your collection. Make many of them in various colors. They are absolutely cute and can be used as keychains, as well.

What You Need:

- ➤ DK/ worsted yarn in color of your choice 50g
- ➤ Black yarn
- o mm crochet hook
- ➤ A pair of 9 mm safety eyes
- ➤ Stuffing
- ➤ Embroidery needle to sew

Body:

1. Use yarn color of your choice
2. R1: 6 sc in MR (6)
3. R2: inc in each st (12)
4. R3: (sc 1, inc 1) *6 (18)
5. R4: (sc 2, inc 1) *6 (24)
6. R5: (sc 3, inc 1) *6 (30)
7. R6: (sc 4, inc 1) *6 (36)
8. R7: (sc 5, inc 1) *6 (42)
9. R8–13: sc in each st (42)
10. R14: BLO (sc 5, dec 1) * 6 (36)
11. R15: (sc 4, dec 1) * 6 (30)
12. You can now attach the eyes between R12 and R13 with 8 sts in between.
13. Using black yarn, sew a mouth on R14.
14. R16: (sc 3, dec 1) *6 (24)
15. R17: (sc 2, dec 1) *6 (18)
16. Stuff the body.
17. R18: (sc 1, dec 1) *6 (12)
18. R19: dec in each st (6)
19. FO leaving a long tail to sew.

Skirt:

1. Using the front loops of R14, attach yarn to any of the sts.
2. Ch 3, 2 dc in the similar st, skip 1 sc, sc in the next, (cut 1 sc, 5 dc in next sc, cut 1 sc, sc in next) * repeat around, 2 dc in first st, sl st to top of ch 3.
3. FO

Tentacles (Make 3 or more):

1. Ch 31, 2 sc in 2nd ch through the hook, 3 sc in every remaining st.
2. FO leaving a long tail to sew.

Assembly:

1. Sew the tentacles to the center of the body base.

11. Bailey the Whale

Bailey is a cute tiny whale with a large heart! This quick-to-make pattern will have you creating several of them in no time. Attach safety eyes or glue on googly eyes for Bailey to stand out. Choose colors of your choice to make Bailey the Whale.

What You Need:

> ➢ DK/worsted yarn in blue and white
> ➢ mm crochet hook
> ➢ A pair of 9 mm safety eyes
> ➢ Stuffing
> ➢ Embroidery needle to sew

Body:

1. Use blue yarn
2. R1: 6 sc in MR (6)
3. R2: inc in each st (12)
4. R3: (sc 1, inc 1) *6 (18)
5. R4: (sc 2, inc 1) *6 (24)
6. R5: (sc 3, inc 1) *6 (30)
7. R6: (sc 4, inc 1) *6 (36)
8. R7: (sc 5, inc 1) *6 (42)
8. .

9. R8: (sc 6, inc 1) *6 (48)
10. R9: (sc 7, inc 1) *6 (54)
11. R10–20: sc in each (54)
12. R21: (sc 7, dec 1) * 6 (48)
13. Change to white yarn.
14. R22: sc in each st (48)
15. R23: (sc 4, dec 1) *8 (40)
16. R24: (sc 2, dec 1) *8 (30)
17. R25: (sc 1, dec 1) *8 (20)
18. Stuff the body.
19. R26: dec in all st (10)
20. R27: dec in all st (5)
21. FO.

Fins (Make 2):

1. Use blue yarn.
2. R1: 6 sc in MR (6)
3. R2: inc in each st (12)
4. R3–6: sc in each st (12)
5. Fold and sc across to close the gap.
6. FO leaving a long tail to sew.
7. Sew the fins to the side of the body at R27.

Tail (Make 2):

1. Use blue yarn.
2. R1: 6 sc in MR (6)
3. R2: inc in each st (12)
4. R3–6: sc in each st (12)
5. Fold and sc across to close the gap.
6. FO
7. Join the two tail pieces at the R1 edge to form a V shape tail. Sew this tail to the body at R27

12. Zippy the Turtle

Another cute pattern those kids will love! Zippy is simple enough to create and can be either made with a single color or multiple colors. Zippy is small in size but packs a punch. You can make him larger in size by just using larger size hooks.

What You Need:

➤ DK/ worsted yarn in colors of your choice (B for color1, W for color2)
➤ 3 – 5 mm crochet hook
➤ A pair of 9 mm safety eyes
➤ Stuffing
➤ Embroidery needle to sew

Body:

1. Use B.
2. R1: 6 sc in MR (6)
3. Change to W.
4. R2: inc in each st (12)
5. Change to B.
6. R3: (sc 1, inc 1) * 6 (18)
7. Change to W.
8. R4: sc in each st (18)
9. Change to B.
10. R5: (sc 2, inc 1) * 6 (24)
11. Change to W.
12. R6: sc in each st (24)
13. Change to B.
14. R7: (sc 3, inc 1) * 6 (30)
15. Change to W.
16. R8: sc in each st (30)
17. Change to B.
18. R9: sc in each st (30)
19. Change to W.
20. R10: sc in each st (30)
21. R11: BLO (sc 3, dec 1) * 6 (24)
22. R12: (sc 2, dec 1) * 6 (18)
23. Stuff the body.
24. R13: (sc 1, dec 1) * 6 (12)
25. R14: dec in each st (6)
26. Fasten off and weave in the ends.

Head:

1. Use white yarn.
2. R1: 6 sc in MR (6)
3. R2: inc in each st (12)
4. R3: (sc 1, inc 1) *6 (18)
5. R4: (sc 2, inc 1) *6 (24)
6. R5–7: sc in each st (24)
7. R8: (sc 2, dec 1) * 6 (18)
8. Attach the eyes at R6.
9. R9: sc in each st (18)
10. R10: (sc 1, dec 1) * 6 (12)
11. FO leaving a long tail to sew.
12. Thrust the head and sew it to the trunk

Legs (Make 4):

1. Use white yarn.
2. R1: 6 sc in MR (6)
3. R2–3: sc in each st (6)
4. FO leaving a long tail to sew. Sew the legs to the body at R11.

Tail:

1. Use white yarn.
2. Ch4, sl st in 2nd ch through the hook, sl st, sc.
3. FO leaving a long tail to sew.
4. Sew the tail to the body at R11.

13.   Cherry the Crab

Cherry is a chubby little crab who's ready to play with you. Make her in your favorite color, but red suits her best. The pattern is a very simple one with a little bit of work on the claws. Try out this amigurumi pattern today.

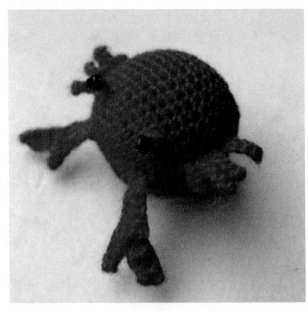

What You Need:

➢ DK/ worsted yarn in the color of your choice
➢ 3 - 5 mm crochet hook
➢ A pair of 6mm safety eyes
➢ Stuffing
➢ Embroidery needle to sew

Body:

1.   R1: 6 sc in MR (6)
2.   R2: inc in each st (12)
3.   R3: (sc 1, inc 1) *6 (18)
4.   R4: (sc 2, inc 1) *6 (24)
5.   R5: (sc 3, inc 1) *6 (30)
6.   R6: (sc 4, inc 1) *6 (36)
7.   R7–8: sc in each st (36)
8.   R9: (sc 4, dec 1) * 6 (30)
9.   R10: (sc 3, dec 1) * 6 (24)
10.   R11: (sc 2, dec 1) * 6 (18)
11.   R12: (sc 1, dec 1) * 6 (12)
12.   R13: dec * 6 (6)
13.   Stuff the body.
14.   Fasten off and weave in the ends.

Legs (Make 4-6):

1.   R1: 5 sc in MR (5)
2.   R2–7: sc in each st (5)
3.   FO leaving a long tail to sew. Sew the legs to the body.

Claws (Make 2):

1.   R1: 4 sc in MR (4)
2.   R2: (sc 1, inc 1) * 2 (6)
3.   R3: (sc 2, inc 1) * 2 (8)
4.   R4: sc in each st (8)
5.   R5: (sc 3, inc 1) * 2 (10)
6.   R6: Ch 3, sc in the 2nd ch from hook, sc in next st, now working on the sts of R5—sc in each st ending with a sc under the triangular piece just made.
7.   R7: sc 5, dec 1, sc 4 (10)
8.   R8: sc 5, dec 1, sc 3 (9)
9.   R9: dec 1, sc 3, dec 1, sc 2 (7)
10.   R10: dec 1, sc 2, dec 1, sc 1 (5)
11.   R11–14: sc in each st (5)
12.   FO leaving a long tail to sew.
13.   Sew the claws on the body. Sew eyes on the body at R7

14. Stef the Clown Fish

Isn't Stef adorable?? Get your supplies and let's get started on this funny little clownfish. With bright orange and white yarn and bulging eyes, Stef is all set to impress you. This is a soft pattern to follow that includes a mix of colours.

What You Need:

- DK/ worsted yarn in orange, white and black
- 3 - 5 mm crochet hook
- A pair of 6mm safety eyes
- Stuffing
- Embroidery needle to sew

Body:

1. Use orange yarn.
2. R1: 6 sc in MR (6)
3. R2: inc in each st (12)
4. R3: (sc 1, inc 1) * 6 (18)
5. R4: (sc 2, inc 1) * 6 (24)
6. R5: (sc 3, inc 1) * 6 (30)
7. R6–7: sc in each st (30)
8. R8: (sc 4, inc 1) * 6 (36)
9. Change to black yarn.
10. Place eyes at R4 with 5 sts in between.
11. R9: sc in each st (36)
12. Change to white yarn.
13. R10–11: sc in each st (36)
14. Change to black yarn.
15. R12: sc in each st (36)
16. Change to orange yarn.
17. R13: sc in each st (36)
18. R14: (sc 4, dec 1) *6 (30)
19. R15–16: sc in each st (30)
20. Change to black.
21. R17: sc in each st (30)
22. Change to white.
23. R18: (sc 3, dec 1) *6 (24)
24. Change to black.
25. R19: sc in each st (24)
26. Change to orange yarn.
27. R20: sc in each st (24)
28. R21: (sc 2, dec 1) * 6 (18)
29. R22: sc in each st (18)
30. Change to black yarn.
31. R23: sc in each st (18)
32. Change to white.
33. R24: sc in each st (18)
34. R25: (sc 1, dec 1) *6 (12)
35. R26: dec * 6 (6)
36. Fasten off and weave in the ends.

Fins (Make 3):

1. Use orange yarn.
2. R1: Ch 7, sc in 2nd ch through the hook, sc in next 5 st
3. R2: Turn, ch1, sc in each st
4. R3: Turn, ch1, sc in first 2 st, dec 1, sc in last 2 sts
5. R4–5: Turn, ch1, sc in each st
6. R6: Turn, ch1, dec 1, sc 1, dec 1
7. FO leaving a long tail to sew.
8. Attach one fin to each side of the body at R12. Attach the third fin to the back of the body.

Dorsal Fin:

1. Use orange yarn.
2. R1: Ch10, sc in 2nd ch through the hook, sc in next 8 st
3. R2: Turn, ch1, sc, hdc, dc, hdc, sc, sc, hdc, hdc, sc
4. R3: Turn, ch1, sc, hdc, hdc, sc, sc, hdc, dc, hdc, sc

5. R4: sc, sc
6. FO leaving a long tail to sew.
7. Attach the fin to the top of the body.

Eyes (Make 2):

1. Use white yarn.
2. R1: 6sc in MR (6)
3. R2: inc in each st (12)
4. R3: (sc 1, inc 1) * 6 (18)
5. FO leaving a long tail to sew.
6. With the wrong side facing out, attach the safety eyes, one inside of each crocheted eye, and sew in place on the body.
7. Sew a mouth using black yarn below the eyes.

15.   Bubbles Fish Out of Water

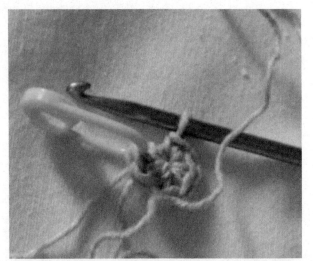
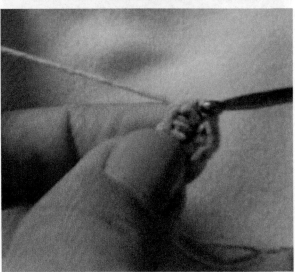

What do you need:

➤ In this pattern, I am using violet cotton yarn.
➤ Hook size N-5.00mm.
➤ Fiber
➤ Safety eyes
➤ Sewing needle
➤ Embroidery yarn
➤ Stitch marker
➤ Stitches Used in this Pattern
➤ Magic ring
➤ Single crochet stitch
➤ Slip stitch

Crochet in joined rounds and don't forget to use a stitch marker at the beginning of each round.

Head and Body:

1. Begin with a magic ring.
2. R1: 6 SC into the magic ring. Join the round by slip stitch into the first stitch, then Ch1

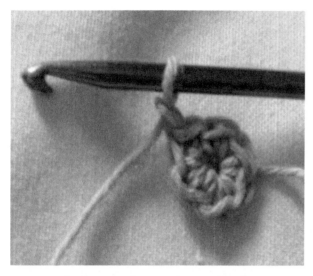

NOTE: The first stitch in each round is the same stitch that you do Sl St in.

3. R2: (INC) X6 = 12 Sts. Join the round by slip stitch into the first stitch, then Ch1.

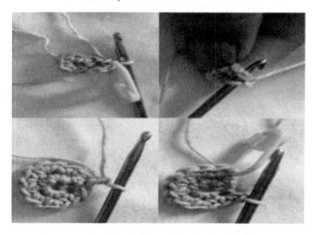

4. R3: (Sc in next 3 St, INC in the next stitch) X3 = 15 Sts. Join the round by slip stitch into the first stitch, then Ch1.

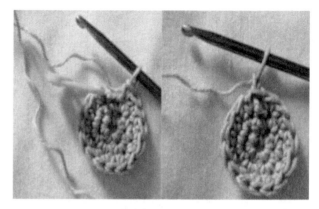

5. R4: (Sc in next 4 St, INC in the next stitch) X3 = 18 Sts. Join the round by slip stitch into the first stitch, then Ch1.

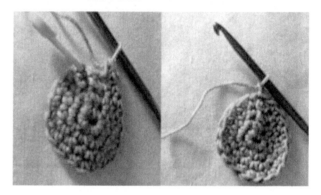

6. R5: (Sc in next 5 St, INC in the next stitch) X3 = 21 Sts. Join the round by slip stitch into the first stitch, then Ch1.

7. R6: (Sc in next 6 St, INC in the next stitch) X3 = 24 Sts. Join the round by slip stitch into the first stitch, then Ch1.

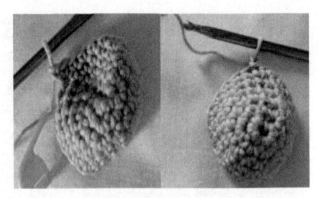

8. R7: Sc around in all 24 St = 24 Sts. Join the round by slip stitch into the first stitch, then Ch1.

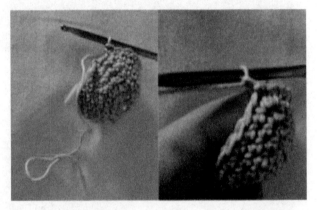

9. R8: (Sc in the next 3 St, INC in the next stitch) X6 = 30 Sts. Join the round by slip stitch into the first stitch, then Ch1.

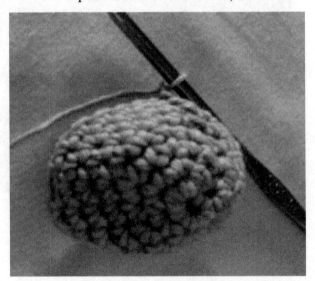

10. R9 to R13: Sc around in all 30 St = 30 Sts. Join each round by slip stitch into the first stitch, then Ch1.

11. R14: (Sc in next 3 St, Dec in the next stitch) X6 = 24 Sts. Join the round by slip stitch into the first stitch, then Ch1.

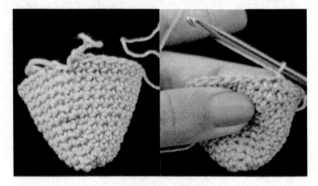

12. R15: (Sc in next 6 St, Dec in the next stitch) X3 = 21 Sts. Join the round by slip stitch into the first stitch, then Ch1.

13. R16: (Sc in next 5 St, Dec in the next stitch) X3 = 18 Sts. Join the round by slip stitch into the first stitch, then Ch1.

14. R17: (Sc in next 4 St, Dec in the next stitch) X3 = 15 Sts. Join the round by slip stitch into the first stitch, then Ch1.

15. R18: (Sc in next 3 St, Dec in the next stitch) X3 = 12 Sts. Join the round by slip stitch into the first stitch, then Ch1.

16. R19: Sc around in all 12 St = 12 Sts. Join each round by slip stitch into the first stitch, then Ch1.
17. Stuff it with fiber.

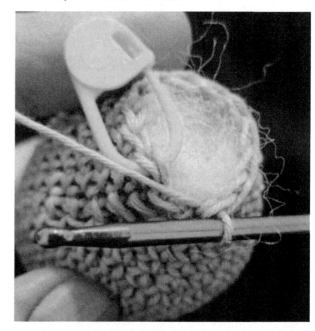

18. Crochet both sides together.
19. 6 Sc, Ch1, fasten off and cut the yarn.

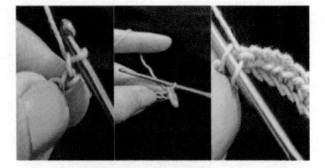

3.   Work the decrease in this way:

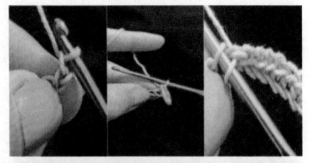

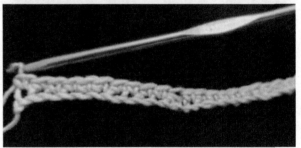

4.   Row 2: Ch 3, from the second chain, work 12 Sc only in the back loop, triple Dec, 11 Sc, Ch 1, and turn your work.

Tail (Make 2):

1.   Ch 25
2.   Row 1: In the second chain from the hook, work 12 Sc in the next 12 stitches, 1 Dec, 10 Sc, Ch1, and turn your work.

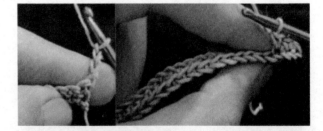

5. Row 3: Ch 2, from the second chain, work 12 Sc only in the back loop, triple Dec, 11 Sc, Ch 1 and turn your work.

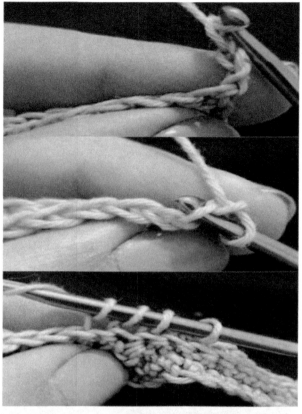

6. Row 4: Ch 2. From the second chain, work12 Sc only in the back loop, triple Dec, 11 Sc, Ch 1, and turn your work.

7. Row 5: Ch 1. From the second chain, work11 Sc only in the back loop, triple Dec, 11 Sc, Ch 1, and turn your work.

8. Row 6: Ch 4, from the second chain work14 Sc only in the back loop, triple Dec, 7 Sc, Ch 1 and turn your work.

9. Row 7: From the second chain, work 6 Sc only in the back loop, triple Dec, 10 Sc, Ch 1, and turn your work.

10. Row 7: From the second chain work9 Sc only in the back loop, triple Dec, 4 Sc, Ch 1 and turn your work.

11. Tighten off and leave a long tail for sewing.

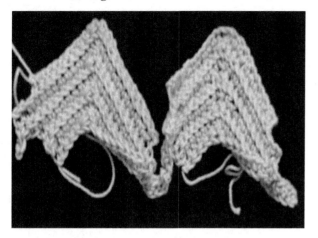

Fins (Make 3):

1. Ch11.

2. Row 1: In the second chain, work 8Sc, triple decrease, Ch1, and turn your work.

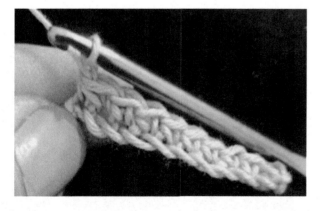

3. Row 2: Work in the back loop. Dec, 7 Sc, Ch1, and turn your work.

4. Row 3: 6 Sc, Dec, Ch1, and turn your work.

5. Row 4: Dec, 5 Sc, Ch1 and turn your work.

6.   Row 5: 4 Sc, Dec, Ch1 and turn your work.

8.   Tighten off and leave a tail for sewing.

7.   Row 6: Dec, 3 Sc, Ch1 and turn your work.

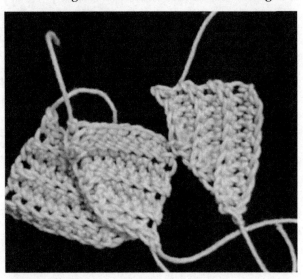

Assembly:

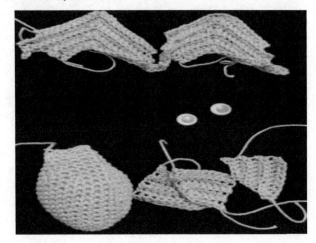

1. Sew the tails and the fins to the body.
2. Put the safety eyes on the front of the eye patch.
3. To make sure that you have placed everything in the right position, use pins to affix each part in its place, then sew them.

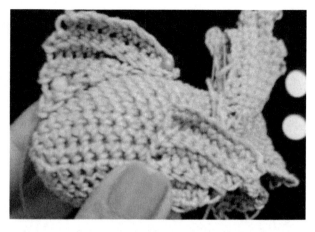

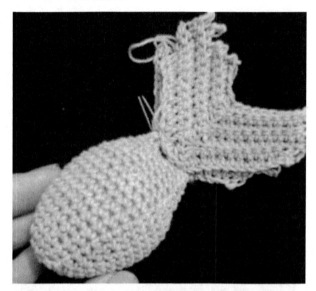

4. Now you have finished the fish.

Now for our cute farm friends which we're sure you'll enjoy crocheting. From a pig to a cow or a sheep to an alpaca, we have a nice group of them here.

Make them in different sizes and you'll have an assortment of barn animals. These incredible patterns are also very simple to make.

Add your choice of yarn colors and choose from soft and snuggly yarn types to make it personal.

16.   Shaun the Sheep

How cute is Shaun the Sheep?! You may choose to sew it in one color or two, and if you want to increase its size, just use a bigger hook size.

What You Need:

- ➢ DK/ worsted yarn in Black and White 3.5mm crochet hook
- ➢ A pair of 6 mm safety eyes
- ➢ Stuffing
- ➢ Embroidery needle to sew

Body:

5. Use white yarn.
6. R1: 6 sc in MR (6)
7. R2: inc in each st (12)
8. R3: (sc 1, inc 1) *6 (18)
9. R4: (sc 2, inc 1) *6 (24)
10. R5: (sc 3, inc 1) *6 (30)
11. R6: (sc 4, inc1) *6 (36)
12. R7–12: sc in each st (36)
13. R13: (sc 4, dec 1) *6 (30)
14. R14: (sc 3, dec 1) *6 (24)
15. R15: (sc 2, dec 1) *6 (18)
16. Stuff the body.
17. R16: (sc 1, dec 1) *6 (12)

18. R17: dec * 6 (6)
19. Fasten off and weave in the ends.

Head:

1. Use black yarn.
2. R1: 6 sc in MR (6)
3. R2: inc in each st (12)
4. R3: (sc 1, inc 1) * 6 (18)
5. R4: (sc 2, inc 1) * 6 (24)
6. R5–7: sc in each st (24)
7. R8: (sc 2, dec 1) * 6 (18)
8. Stuff the head.
9. R9: (sc 1, dec 1) * 6 (12)
10. R11: (dec 1) * 6 (6)
11. Fasten off and weave in the ends.

Legs (Make 4)

1. Use black yarn
2. R1: 6 sc in MR (6)
3. R2: inc in each st (12)
4. R3–5: sc in each st (12)
5. Thrust the legs and sew them to the body.

Tail:

1. Use black yarn
2. R1: 6 sc in MR (6)
3. R2: inc in each st (12)
4. R3: (sc 1, inc 1) * 6 (18)
5. Thrust the tail and sew to the body.

Ears (Make 2)

1. Use black yarn.
2. R1: 6 sc in MR (6)
3. R2: inc in each st (12)
4. FO leaving a long tail to sew.
5. Sew the ears to the body.

17. Penny the Pig

A farm wouldn't be complete without Penny the Pig. I chose pink for Penny, but you can choose whatever color you prefer.

What You Need:

- ➤ DK/ worsted yarn in pink or color of your choice 50g
  - ➤ Black yarn
  - ➤ 3,5 mm crochet hook
  - ➤ A pair of 6 mm safety eyes
  - ➤ Stuffing
  - ➤ Embroidery needle to sew

Head & Body:

1. R1: 6 sc in MR (6)
2. R2: (inc 1, sc 1) * 3 (9)
3. R3: (BLO) sc in each st (9)
4. R4: sc in each st (9)
5. R5: (inc 1, sc 2) *3 (12)
6. R6: sc in each st (12)
7. R7: (inc 1, sc 1) *6 (18)
8. R8:(inc1, sc2) *6 (24)
9. R9:(inc1, sc3) *6 (30)
10. R10: (inc 1, sc 9) * 3 (33)
11. You can now attach safety eyes between R7 and R8 with 6 sts in between.
12. R11–19: sc in each st (33)
13. R20: (dec 1, sc 9) * 3 (30)
14. R21: (dec 1, sc 3) * 6 (24)
15. Stuff the pig now and continue stuffing as you go.
16. R22: (dec 1, sc 2) * 6 (18)
17. R23: (dec 1, sc 1) * 6 (12)
18. R24: dec * 6 (6)
19. Stuff well. Fasten off and weave in the ends.

Tail:

1. Chain 20.
2. Sl st in the second ch through the hook and in the remaining 18 chains. FO leaving a long tail for sewing.
3. Fix the tail to the body at the center of R24.

Legs (Make 4):

1. R1: 6 sc in MR (6)
2. R2–3: sc in each st (6)
3. Sl st in next st
4. FO leaving a long tail for sewing. Stuff the leg.
5. Once you create all 4 legs, sew on the two legs at R9 with 4 sts in between the two legs at R14 with 6 sts in between.

Ears (Make 2):

1. R1: 3 sc in MR, ch1, Turn (3)
2. R2: 2 sc in one of the 3 sts (6)
3. R3: 2 sc in MR (8)
4. FO leaving a long tail for sewing.
5. Sew the ears at R9 with 4 sts in between.

Finishing:

1. Using black yarn, make small straight stitches for nostrils at R2.

18.   Lulu the Alpaca

Lulu the alpaca is soft, fuzzy, cuddly and one adorable animal from South America. Add soft colors to Lulu and you'll have the best cuddly toy around.

What You Need:

- ➤ DK/ worsted yarn in the color of your choice
- ➤ 3.5 mm crochet hook
- ➤ A pair of 4 mm safety eyes
- ➤ Stuffing
- ➤ Embroidery needle to sew

Body:

1. R1: 8 sc in MR (8)
2. R2: inc in each st (16)
3. R3: (sc in 1 st, sc inc 1) * 8 (24)
4. R4: (sc in 2 sts, sc in c 1) *8 (32)
5. R5: (sc in 3 sts, sc in c1) *8 (40)
6. R6–26: sc in each st (40)
7. R27: (sc in 3 sts, sc dec 1) * 8 (32)
8. R28: (sc in 2 sts, sc dec 1) * 8 (24)
9. R29: (sc in 1 st, sc dec 1) * 8 (16)
10. Stuff the body
11. R30: sc dec * 8 (8)
12. Fasten off and weave in the ends.

Head:

1. R1: 8 sc in MR (8)
2. R2: inc in each st (16)
3. R3: (sc in 1 st, sc inc 1) * 8 (24)
4. R4: (sc in 2 sts, sc inc 1) * 8 (32)
5. R5–14: sc in each st (32)
6. Attach safety eyes at R7
7. R16: (sc in 2 sts, sc dec 1) *8 (24)
8. R17–27: sc in each st (24)

9. R28: (sc in 1 st, sc dec 1) *8 (16)
10. Stuff the head
11. FO leaving a long tail to sew.
12. Attach the head to the body.

Mouth:

1. R1: 6 sc in MR (6)
2. R2: inc in each st (12)
3. R3: (sc in 1 st, sc inc 1) * 6 (18)
4. R4–5: sc in each st (18)
5. Stuff the mouth.
6. FO leaving a long tail to sew.
7. Attach the mouth to the head.

Legs (Make 4):

1. R1: 6 sc in MR (6)
2. R2: inc in each st (12)
3. R3: (sc in 1 st, sc inc 1) * 6 (18)
4. R4–10: sc in each st (18)
5. R11: (sc in 2 sts, sc inc 1) *6 (24)
6. R12: sc in each st (24)
7. Stuff the legs.
8. FO leaving a long tail to sew.
9. Attach the legs to the body.

Ears (Make 2):

1. R1: 3 sc in MR (3)
2. R2: inc in each st (6)
3. R3–5: sc in each st (6)
4. FO leaving a long tail to sew.
5. Attach the ears to the head.

For the hair:

1. Cut four pieces of yarn 4 inches in length and attach them to the front of the head in a knot. Open up each strand of yarn to give a fluffier look.

For the tail:

1. Cut four pieces of yarn 4 inches in length and attach to the back of the body in a knot. Open up each strand of yarn to give a fluffier look.

19.   Daisy the Duck

Daisy is a colorful duck and she's ready to get quacking with you. Experiment with different colors to achieve a gorgeous result.

What You Need:

➢ DK/ worsted yarn in colors of your choice
➢ 3 mm crochet hook
➢ A pair of 4 mm safety eyes
➢ Stuffing
➢ Embroidery needle to sew

Head:

1. R1: 6 sc in MR (6)
2. R2: sc inc in each st (12)
3. R3: (sc in 1 st, sc inc 1) * 6 (18)
4. R4: (sc in 2 sts, sc inc 1) * 6 (24)
5. R5: (sc in 3 sts, sc inc 1) * 6 (30)
6. R6: (sc in 4 sts, sc inc 1) * 6 (36)
7. R7: (sc in 5 sts, sc inc 1) * 6 (42)
8. R8: (sc in 6 sts, sc inc 1) * 6 (48)
9. R9–19: sc in each st (48)
10. Attach eyes at R14 with 8 sts in between.
11. R20: (sc in 6 sts, sc dec 1) *6 (42)
12. R21: (sc in 5 sts, sc dec 1) *6 (36)
13. R22: (sc in 4 sts, sc dec 1) *6 (30)
14. R23: (sc in 3 sts, sc dec 1) *6 (24)
15. R24: (sc in 2 sts, sc dec 1) *6 (18)
16. R25: (sc in 1 st, sc dec 1) * 6 (12)
17. R26: (sc dec) * 6 (6)

18. Stuff the head.
19. Fasten and weave in the ends.

Body:

1. R1: 6 sc in MR (6)
2. R2: sc inc in each st (12)
3. R3: (sc in 1 st, sc inc 1) * 6 (18)
4. R4: (sc in 2 sts, sc inc 1) *6 (24)
5. R5: (sc in 3 sts, sc inc 1) *6 (30)
6. R6: (sc in 4 sts, sc inc 1) *6 (36)
7. R7–10: sc in each st (36)
8. R11: (sc in 4 sts, sc dec 1) *6 (30)
9. R12–13: sc in each st (30)
10. R14: (sc in 3 sts, sc dec 1) *6 (24)
11. R15–17: sc in each st (24)
12. R18: (sc in 2 sts, sc dec 1) *6 (18)
13. Stuff the body.
14. FO leaving a long tail to sew.

Wings (Make 2):

1. R1: 6 sc into MR (6)
2. R2: sc in each st (6)
3. R3: inc in each st (12)
4. R4–9: sc in each st (12)
5. Fold the piece in half and make 6 sc to close.
6. FO leaving a long tail to sew.
7. Sew the wings to the face of the body.

Feet (Make 2):

1. R1: Ch 4
2. R2: sc in 3 st, ch1, turn (3)
3. R3: sc inc 1, sc, sc inc 1, ch1, turn (5)
4. R4: sc inc 1, sc in 3 sts, sc inc 1, ch1, turn (7)
5. R5: sc inc 1, sc in 5 sts, sc inc 1, ch1, turn (9)
6. R6: sl st, (hdc, ch1, sl st, sl st) * 2, hdc, ch1, sl st
7. Fasten off and weave in the ends.
8. Sew the feet to the rear of the body.

Beak:

1. R1: ch 5, inc in 2nd ch from hook, sc in 2 sts, 3 sc in next st, now working behind the stitches, sc in 2 sts, sc in 1st st (10)
2. R2: sc in each st (10)
3. R3: sc inc 1, sc in 4 sts, sc inc 1, sc in 4 sts (12)
4. R4: sc, sc inc 1, sc in 5 sts, sc inc 1, sc in 4 sts (14)
5. R5: sc, sc, sc inc 1, sc in 6 sts, sc inc 1, sc in 4 sts (16)
6. Stuff the beak lightly.
7. FO leaving a long tail to sew.
8. Sew the beak to the face of the head.

Hair:

1. Cut two strands of yarn 3 inches long. Fold each in half and, using a 1.5 mm hook, attach it to the top of the head by making a knot. Put the needle on any of the sc on the first row of the head, pick the yarn and pull out and make a sl st. Trim the yarn to about 1 inch.

Our wild animal collection are made up of some of the most majestic animals in the world.

We give you some simple patterns with which to create these stunning wild animals.

You will find the patterns to be similar to our previous animal patterns, with a few particular changes here and there, which makes it another collection for you to have as you master the art of amigurumi.

Browse through this book and find your favorite wild animal and let the magic of crochet begin. Your creation will surely be loved by all.

20.   Hugo the Hippo

Hugo the Hippo is a simple yet fun pattern that you can create easily. With a large head, he demands attention from everyone around him. Try out various colors of yarn to make him colorful and fun to play with.

What You Need:

- ➤ DK/ worsted yarn in the color of your choice
- ➤ Pink yarn
- ➤ 4 mm crochet hook
- ➤ A pair of 6mm safety eyes
- ➤ Stuffing
- ➤ Embroidery needle to sew

Head:

2. Ch 4
3. R1: 2 sc in 2nd ch through the hook, sc, 3 sc in last ch
4. Working along the back of the chain, sc, sc (8)
5. R2: inc 1 in first sc, inc 1, sc, inc 1, inc 1, inc 1, sc, inc 1 (14)
6. R3: inc 1 in first sc, inc 1, sc in next 4 sc, inc 1, inc 1, inc 1, sc in the next four sc, inc 1. (20)
7. R4–7: sc in each sc (20) R8:(dec 1, dec 1, sc in next 6 sc) *2 (16)
8. R9: (dec 1, sc in next 6 sc) * 2 (14)
9. R10-11: sc in each st (14)
10. Stuff the body.

11. R12: (dec 1, sc 2) * around and end with dec 1 in last 2 sc (10)
12. R13: dec in each st (5)
13. Fasten off and weave in the ends.

Body:

1. R1: 5 sc in MR (5)
2. R2: inc in each st (10)
3. R3: (sc 1, inc 1) *5 (15)
4. R4: (sc 2, inc 1) *5 (20)
5. R5: (sc 3, inc 1) *5 (25)
6. R6–8: sc in each st (25)
7. R9: (sc 3, dec 1) * 5 (20)
8. R10–12: sc in each st (20)
9. R13: (dec 1, sc 2) * 5 (15)
10. FO leaving a long tail to sew. Sew head to the body.

Ears (Make 2):

1. R1: 6 sc in MR (6)
2. R2: inc in each st (12)
3. FO leaving a long tail to sew.
4. Sew ears to head.
5. Using pink yarn, embroider straight and stitch for nostrils.

Legs (Make 4):

1. R1: 6 sc in MR (6)
2. R2–4: sc in each st (6)
3. FO leaving a long tail to sew. Sew the legs to the body.

Tail:

1. Ch 4, sl st in 2nd ch through the hook, sc, sc.
2. Fasten off and weave in the ends.
3. Sew tail to body.

21.   Nano the Rhino

This rhino pattern is similar to the hippo pattern given above. With the addition of the horns, the pattern can be changed to that of a rhino. So, try your skill and enjoy this simple pattern.

What You Need:

- ➤ DK/ worsted yarn in the color of your choice
- ➤ Dark Grey yarn
- ➤ 4 mm crochet hook
- ➤ A pair of 6 mm safety eyes
- ➤ Stuffing
- ➤ Embroidery needle to sew

Head:

1. Ch 4
2. R1: 2 sc in 2nd ch through the hook, sc, 3 sc in last ch
3. Working along the back of the chain, sc, sc (8)
4. R2: inc 1 in first sc, inc 1, sc, inc 1, inc 1, inc 1, sc, inc 1 (14)
5. R3: inc 1 in first sc, inc 1, sc in next 4 sc, inc 1, inc 1, inc 1, sc in the next four sc, inc 1. (20)
6. R4–7: sc in each sc (20)
7. R8: (dec 1, dec 1, sc in next 6 sc) *2 (16)
8. R9: (dec 1, sc in next 6 sc) * 2 (14)
9. R10–11: sc in each st (14)
10. Stuff the body.
11. R12: (dec 1, sc 2) * around and end with dec 1 in last 2 sc (10)
12. R13: dec in each st (5)
13. Fasten off and weave in the ends.

Horns:

1. Use dark grey yarn

Small:

1. R1: 3 sc in MR (3)
2. R2: inc in each st (6)
3. R3: (sc 2, inc 1) *2 (8)
4. R4: sc in each st (8)

Big:

1. R1: 3 sc in MR (3)
2. R2: inc in each st (6)
3. R3: (sc 2, inc 1) *2 (8)
4. R4: (sc 3, inc 1) *2 (10)
5. R5: sc in each st (10)
6. Sew both the horns on the head.

Body:

1. R1: 5 sc in MR (5)
2. R2: inc in each st (10)
3. R3: (sc 1, inc 1) * 5 (15)
4. R4: (sc 2, inc 1) * 5 (20)
5. R5: (sc 3, inc 1) * 5 (25)
6. R6–8: sc in each st (25)
7. R9: (sc 3, dec 1) * 5 (20)
8. R10–12: sc in each st (20)
9. R13: (dec 1, sc 2) * 5 (15)
10. FO leaving a long tail to sew.
11. Sew head to the body.

Ears (Make 2):

1. R1: 6 sc in MR (6)
2. R2: inc in each st (12)
3. FO leaving a long tail to sew. Sew ears to head.
4. Using pink yarn, embroider straight and stitch for nostrils.

Legs (Make 4):

1. Use dark grey yarn
2. R1: 6 sc in MR (6)
3. R2: sc in each st (6)
4. Change to body-color
5. R3–4: sc in each st (6)
6. FO leaving a long tail to sew.
7. Sew the legs to the body.

Tail:

1. Ch 4, sl st in 2nd ch through the hook, sc, sc.

22.   Ella the Elephant

Ella, the elephant, is a fun wild animal that you can enjoy. Her cute little trunk makes her very inquisitive. You can make her in different colors and have fun with this pattern.

What You Need:

➢ DK/ worsted yarn in the color of your choice
➢ 4 mm crochet hook
➢ A pair of 6 mm safety eyes
➢ Stuffing
➢ Embroidery needle to sew

Head:

1. R1: 6 sc in MR (6)
2. R2: sc inc in each st (12)
3. R3: (sc in 1 st, sc inc 1) * 6 (18)
4. R4:(sc in 2 sts, sc inc 1) *6 (24)
5. R5: (sc in 3 sts, sc inc 1) *6 (30)
6. R6: (sc in 4 sts, sc inc 1) *6 (36)
7. R7: (sc in 5 sts, sc inc 1) *6 (42)
8. R8–13: sc in each st (42)
9. Attach eyes to the head at R5
10. R14: (sc in 5 sts, sc dec 1) * 6 (36)
11. R15: (sc in 4 sts, sc dec 1) * 6 (30)
12. R16: (sc in 3 sts, sc dec 1) * 6 (24)
13. R17: (sc in 2 sts, sc dec 1) * 6 (18)
14. Stuff the head.

2. Fasten off and weave in the ends.
3. Sew tail to body.

15. R18: (sc in 1 st, sc dec 1) * 6 (12)
16. R19: dec in each st (6)
17. Fasten off and weave in the ends.

Trunk:

1. R1: 6 sc in MR (6)
2. R2: sc in each st (6)
3. R3: sc in 3 sts, sl st in 3 sts (6)
4. R4: (sc in 1 sts, sc inc 1) *3 (9)
5. R5–6: sc in each st (9)
6. R7: (sc in 2 sts, sc inc 1) *3 (12)
7. R8–9: sc in 2 sts, sl st in 6 sts, sc in 4 sts (12)
8. R10: sc in 4 sts, sl st in 4 sts, sc in 4 sts (12)
9. FO leaving a long tail to sew.
10. Sew the trunk to the front of the head.

Body:

1. R1: 6 sc in MR (6)
2. R2: sc inc in each st (12)
3. R3: (sc in 1 st, sc inc 1) * 6 (18)
4. R4: (sc in 2 sts, sc inc 1) *6 (24)
5. R5: (sc in 3 sts, sc inc 1) *6 (30)
6. R6: (sc in 4 sts, sc inc 1) *6 (36)
7. R7–12: sc in each st (36)
8. R13: (sc in 4 sts, sc dec 1) * 6 (30)
9. R14: (sc in 3 sts, sc dec 1) * 6 (24)
10. R15: (sc in 2 sts, sc dec 1) * 6 (18)
11. Stuff the body.
12. R16: (sc in 1 st, sc dec 1) * 6 (12)
13. R17: dec in each st (6)
14. Fasten off and weave in the ends.
15. Sew the head to the body.

Arms (Make 2):

1. R1: 6 sc in MR (6)
2. R2: sc inc in each st (12)
3. R3–4: sc in each st (12)
4. R5: (sc in 4 sts, sc dec 1) *2 (10)

5. R6–7: sc in each st (10)
6. R8: (sc in 3 sts, sc dec 1) *2 (8)
7. R9: sc in each st (8)
8. Stuff lightly.
9. FO leaving a long tail to sew.
10. Fix the arms to the sides of the body.

Legs (Make 2):

1. R1: 6 sc in MR (6)
2. R2: sc inc in each st (12)
3. R3–8: sc in each st (12)
4. R9: (sc in 1 st, sc dec 1) * 4 (8)
5. Stuff lightly.
6. FO leaving a long tail to sew.
7. Fix the legs to the sides of the body.

Ears (Make 2):

1. R1: 6 sc in MR (6)
2. R2: sc inc in each st (12)
3. R3: (sc in 1 st, sc inc 1) * 6 (18)
4. R4: (sc in 2 sts, sc inc 1) * 6 (24)
5. R5–7: sc in each st (24)
6. R8: (sc in 6 sts, sc dec 1) *3 (21)
7. R9: (sc in 5 sts, sc dec 1) *3 (18)
8. FO leaving a long tail to sew.
9. Attach the ears to the head.

Tail:

Ch 10 and fasten off, leaving a 1-inch tail. Cut four strands of 3 inches in length and attach it along with the Ch 10 to the end of the tail. Open up the strands to make it look fluffier.

23.   Honey the Bear

This pattern is simple to learn. With this template, you may customize it to fit a variety of styles. So, get out your hook and yarn and make this beautiful bear. Make it as a present or just to add to your personal collection.

What You Need:

➢ DK/ worsted yarn in the color of your choice
➢ 4 mm crochet hook
➢ A pair of 6 mm safety eyes
➢ Stuffing
➢ Embroidery needle to sew

Head:

1. R1: 6 sc in MR (6)
2. R2: sc inc in each st (12)
3. R3: (sc in 1 st, sc inc 1) * 6 (18)
4. R4: (sc in 2 sts, sc inc 1) *6 (24)
5. R5: (sc in 3 sts, sc inc 1) *6 (30)
6. R6: (sc in 4 sts, sc inc 1) *6 (36)
7. R7: (sc in 5 sts, sc inc 1) *6 (42)
8. R8–13: sc in each st (42)
9. Attach eyes to the head at R9
10. R14: (sc in 5 sts, sc dec 1) * 6 (36)
11. R15: (sc in 4 sts, sc dec 1) * 6 (30)
12. R16: (sc in 3 sts, sc dec 1) * 6 (24)
13. R17: (sc in 2 sts, sc dec 1) * 6 (18)
14. Stuff the head.
15. R18: (sc in 1 st, sc dec 1) * 6 (12)
16. R19: dec in each st (6)
17. Fasten off and weave in the ends.

Mouth:

1. R1: 6 sc in MR (6)
2. R2: sc inc in each st (12)
3. R3: (sc in 1 st, sc inc 1) * 6 (18)
4. R4–6: sc in each st (18)
5. R7: (sc in 1 st, sc dec 1) * 6 (12)

6. Stuff the mouth.
7. FO leaving a long tail to sew.
8. Sew the mouth to the front of the head. With black yarn sew straight stitch on R2.

Body:

1. R1: 6 sc in MR (6)
2. R2: sc inc in each st (12)
3. R3: (sc in 1 st, sc inc 1) * 6 (18)
4. R4: (sc in 2 sts, sc inc 1) *6 (24)
5. R5: (sc in 3 sts, sc inc 1) *6 (30)
6. R6: (sc in 4 sts, sc inc 1) *6 (36)
7. R7–12: sc in each st (36)
8. R13: (sc in 4 sts, sc dec 1) * 6 (30)
9. R14: (sc in 3 sts, sc dec 1) * 6 (24)
10. R15: (sc in 2 sts, sc dec 1) * 6 (18)
11. Stuff the body.
12. R16: (sc in 1 st, sc dec 1) * 6 (12)
13. R17: dec in each st (6)
14. Fasten off and weave in the ends.
15. Sew the head to the body.

Arms (Make 2):

1. R1: 6 sc in MR (6)
2. R2: sc inc in each st (12)
3. R3–4: sc in each st (12)
4. R5: (sc in 4 sts, sc dec 1) *2 (10)
5. R6–7: sc in each st (10)

6. R8: (sc in 3 sts, sc dec 1) *2 (8)
7. R9: sc in each st (8)
8. Stuff lightly.
9. FO leaving a long tail to sew.
10. Fix the arms to the sides of the body.

Legs (Make 2):

1. R1: 6 sc in MR (6)
2. R2: sc inc in each st (12)
3. R3–8: sc in each st (12)
4. R9: (sc in 1 st, sc dec 1) * 4 (8)
5. Stuff lightly.
6. FO leaving a long tail to sew.
7. Fix the legs to the sides of the body.

Ears (Make 2):

1. R1: 6 sc in MR (6)
2. R2: sc inc in each st (12)
3. R3: (sc in 1 st, sc inc 1) * 6 (18)
4. R4: (sc in 2 sts, sc inc 1) * 6 (24)
5. R5–7: sc in each st (24)
6. R8:(sc in 6 sts, sc dec 1) *3 (21)
7. R9: (sc in 5 sts, sc dec 1) *3 (18)
8. FO leaving a long tail to sew.
9. Attach the ears to the head.

24.   Comet the Reindeer

Have some Christmas cheer with Comet, the reindeer? Make him in festive colors to enjoy the season. You can choose to accessorize him with scarfs and bows as well. He will surely be a great addition to the family. Kids and adults love to have some cheerful holiday spirit all year round.

What You Need:

➢ DK/ worsted yarn in the color of your choice
➢ White and red yarn
➢ 4 mm crochet hook
➢ A pair of 6mm safety eyes
➢ Stuffing
➢ Embroidery needle to sew

Head:

1. R1: 6 sc in MR (6)
2. R2: sc inc in each st (12)
3. R3: (sc in 1 st, sc inc 1) * 6 (18)
4. R4: (sc in 2 sts, sc inc 1) *6 (24)
5. R5: (sc in 3 sts, sc inc 1) *6 (30)

6. R6: (sc in 4 sts, sc inc 1) *6 (36)
7. R7: (sc in 5 sts, sc inc 1) *6 (42)
8. R8-13: sc in each st (42)
9. Attach eyes to the head at R9
10. R14: (sc in 5 sts, sc dec 1) * 6 (36)
11. R15: (sc in 4 sts, sc dec 1) * 6 (30)
12. R16: (sc in 3sts, sc dec 1) * 6 (24)
13. R17: (sc in 2 sts, sc dec 1) * 6 (18)
14. Stuff the head.
15. R18: (sc in 1 st, sc dec 1) * 6 (12)
16. R19: dec in each st (6)
17. Fasten off and weave in the ends.

Mouth:

1. With white yarn.
2. R1: 6 sc in MR (6)
3. R2: sc inc in each st (12)
4. R3: (sc in 1 st, sc inc 1) * 6 (18)
5. R4–6: sc in each st (18)
6. R7: (sc in 1 st, sc dec 1) * 6 (12)
7. Stuff the mouth.
8. FO leaving a long tail to sew.
9. Sew the mouth to the front of the head.
10. With red yarn, sew a nose from R1 to R3.

Body:

1. R1: 6 sc in MR (6)
2. R2: sc inc in each st (12)
3. R3: (sc in 1 st, sc inc 1) * 6 (18)
4. R4: (sc in 2 sts, sc inc 1) *6 (24)
5. R5: (sc in 3 sts, sc inc 1) *6 (30)
6. R6: (sc in 4 sts, sc inc 1) *6 (36)
7. R7–12: sc in each st (36)
8. R13: (sc in 4 sts, sc dec 1) * 6 (30)
9. R14: (sc in 3 sts, sc dec 1) * 6 (24)
10. R15: (sc in 2sts, sc dec 1) * 6 (18)
11. Stuff the body.
12. R16: (sc in 1 st, sc dec 1) * 6 (12)
13. R17: dec in each st (6)
14. Fasten off and weave in the ends.

15. Sew the head to the body.

Legs (Make 4):

1. R1: 6 sc in MR (6)
2. R2: inc in each st (12)
3. R3–7: sc in each st (12)
4. FO leaving a long tail to sew.
5. Thrust the legs and sew them to the body.

Antlers (Make 2):

Long part:

1. R1: 6 sc in MR (6)
2. R2: inc in each st (12)
3. R3–7: sc in each st (12)
4. FO leaving a long tail to sew.

Short part:

1. R1: 6 sc in MR (6)
2. R2: inc in each st (12)
3. R3–5: sc in each st (12)
4. FO leaving a long tail to sew.
5. Now, join one short part to one long part to form a Y shape. Attach the two completed antlers to the top of the head.

Ears (Make 2):

1. R1: 6 sc in MR (6)
2. R2: inc in each st (12)
3. R3–4: sc in each st (12)
4. FO leaving a long tail to sew.
5. Fix the ears to the top of the head.

Scarf:

1. Use red yarn.
2. Ch 30.
3. Hdc in each of the ch.
4. Fasten off and weave in the ends.
5. Place the scarf around the neck and secure it with a knot.

25.   Dave the Tiger

Dave is a cool-looking tiger that you can easily crochet. Make him a happy tiger by adding a large smile to his face. With large buttons or safety eyes, Dave the Tiger comes to life!

What You Need:

- ➢ DK/ worsted yarn in the color of your choice
- ➢ White and black yarn
- ➢ 4 mm crochet hook
- ➢ A pair of 6 mm safety eyes
- ➢ Stuffing
- ➢ Embroidery needle to sew

Head:

1. R1: 6 sc in MR (6)
2. R2: sc inc in each st (12)
3. R3: (sc in 1 st, sc inc 1) * 6 (18)
4. R4: (sc in 2 sts, sc inc 1) *6 (24)
5. R5: (sc in 3 sts, sc inc 1) *6 (30)
6. R6: (sc in 4 sts, sc inc 1) *6 (36)
7. R7: (sc in 5 sts, sc inc 1) *6 (42)
8. R8: sc in each st (42)
9. R9: (sc in 6 sts, sc inc 1) *6 (48)
10. R10: sc in each st (48)
11. R11: (sc in 7 sts, sc inc 1) * 6 (54)
12. R12–17: sc in each st (54)
13. R18: (sc in 7 sts, sc dec 1) * 6 (48)
14. R19: (sc in 6 sts, sc dec 1) * 6 (42)
15. R20: (sc in 5 sts, sc dec 1) * 6 (36)
16. R21: (sc in 4 sts, sc dec 1) * 6 (30)
17. R22: (sc in 3 sts, sc dec 1) * 6 (24)
18. Stuff the head.
19. FO leaving a long tail to sew.

Mouth:

1. R1: 6 sc in MR (6)
2. R2: sc inc in each st (12)
3. R3: (sc in 1 st, sc inc 1) * 6 (18)
4. R4: (sc in 2 sts, sc inc 1) *6 (24)
5. R5: (sc in 3 sts, sc inc 1) *6 (30)
6. FO leaving a long tail to sew.
7. With black yarn, sew a nose and lips to the mouth. Attach the mouth to the head. With black yarn add whiskers. Attach the safety eyes just above the mouth. Using black yarn, you can add stripes by sewing straight stitches at equal intervals at the back of the head.

Body:

1. R1: 6 sc in MR (6)
2. R2: sc inc in each st (12)
3. R3: (sc in 1 st, sc inc 1) * 6 (18)
4. R4: (sc in 2 sts, sc inc 1) *6 (24)
5. R5: (sc in 3 sts, sc inc 1) *6 (30)
6. R6–7: sc in each st (30)
7. CC black yarn
8. R8: sc in each st (30)
9. CC main color
10. R9-10: sc in each st (30)
11. CC black yarn
12. R11: (sc in 3 sts, sc dec 1) * 6 (24)
13. CC main color
14. R12–14: sc in each st (24)
15. Stuff the body.
16. Using the yarn left from the head, sew the body and head together at the open ends.

Legs (Make 2):

1. R1: ch 4, sc in 2nd ch through the hook, sc, 3 sc in next st, (working backwards) sc, 2 sc in last st.
2. R2: sc inc 1, sc, (sc inc 1) * 3, sc, (sc inc 1) * 2
3. R3: scinc1, sc, sc, (sc i c 1, sc) *3, sc, (sc inc 1, sc) *2
4. R4: sc in each st
5. R5: sc in 5 sts, (sc dec 1, sc in 2 sts) * 3, sc in 3 sts
6. R6: sc in 5 sts, (sc dec 1, sc in 1 st) * 3, sc in 3 sts
7. R7–8: sc in each st
8. FO leaving a long tail to sew.
9. Thrust the legs and attach them to the body.
10. Using black yarn, you can add stripes by sewing straight stitches at equal intervals.

Arms (Make 2):

1. R1: 6 sc in MR (6)
2. R2: sc inc in each st (12)

3. R3–9: sc in each st (12)
4. FO leaving a long tail to sew.
5. Thrust the arms and attach them to the body.
6. Using black yarn, you can add stripes by sewing straight stitches at equal intervals.

Tail:

1. R1: 6 sc in MR (6)
2. R2: (sc in 1 st, sc inc 1) * 3 (9)
3. R3–12: sc in each st (9)
4. FO leaving a long tail to sew.
5. Thrust the tail and attach it to the body.

Ears (Make 2):

1. R1: 6 sc in MR (6)
2. R2: sc inc in each st (12)
3. R3: (sc in 3 sts, sc inc 1) * 3 (15)
4. R4–5: sc in each st (15)
5. FO leaving a long tail to sew.
6. Attach to the head.

26.   Zen the Panda

This panda will be a great and adorable addition to your collection. With those cute looks, Zen is sure to impress everyone around. This black and white Panda is something you can easily create.

What You Need:

➢ DK/ worsted yarn in black and white
➢ 4 mm crochet hook
➢ A pair of 6 mm safety eyes
➢ Stuffing
➢ Embroidery needle to sew

Head:

1. Use white yarn.
2. R1: 6 sc in MR (6)
3. R2: sc inc in each st (12)
4. R3: (sc in 1 st, sc inc 1) * 6 (18)
5. R4: (sc in 2 sts, sc inc 1) * 6 (24)
6. R5: (sc in 3 sts, sc inc 1) * 6 (30)
7. R6: (sc in 4 sts, sc inc 1) * 6 (36)
8. R7: (sc in 5 sts, sc inc 1) * 6 (42)
9. R8: sc in each st (42)
10. R9: (sc in 6 sts, sc inc 1) * 6 (48)
11. R10: sc in each st (48)
12. R11: (sc in 7 sts, sc inc 1) * 6 (54)
13. R12-17: sc in each st (54)
14. R18: (sc in 7 sts, sc dec 1) * 6 (48)
15. R19: (sc in 6 sts, sc dec 1) * 6 (42)
16. R20: (sc in 5 sts, sc dec 1) * 6 (36)
17. R21: (sc in 4 sts, sc dec 1) * 6 (30)

18. R22: (sc in 3 sts, sc dec 1) * 6 (24)
19. Stuff the head.
20. FO leaving a long tail to sew.

Mouth:

1. R1: 6 sc in MR (6)
2. R2: sc inc in each st (12)
3. R3: (sc in 1 st, sc inc 1) * 6 (18)
4. R4: (sc in 2 sts, sc inc 1) * 6 (24)
5. R5–6: sc in each st (24) FO leaving a long tail to sew.
6. With black yarn, sew a nose and lips to the mouth. Stuff the mouth and attach the mouth to the head.

Eye Patch (Make 2):

1. Use black yarn
2. R1:Ch4, sc in 2 nd ch from hook, sc, sc inc 1, sc, sc inc 1
3. R2: sc inc 1, sc in 3 sts, sc inc 1, sc inc 1, sc in 3 sts, sc inc 1
4. R3: sc, sc inc 1, sc in 2 sts, hdc, hdc inc 1, sc in 2 sts, hdc inc 1, hdc, sc in 2 sts, sc inc 1, sc
5. FO leaving a long tail to sew. Attach to the head.
6. Attach safety eyes on the eye patch.

Body:

1. Use white yarn.
2. R1: 6 sc in MR (6)
3. R2: sc inc in each st (12)
4. R3: (sc in 1 st, sc inc 1) * 6 (18)
5. R4: (sc in 2 sts, sc inc 1) * 6 (24)
6. R5: (sc in 3 sts, sc inc 1) * 6 (30)
7. R6–10: sc in each st (30)
8. R11: (sc in 3 sts, sc dec 1) * 6 (24)
9. CC black yarn
10. R12–14: sc in each st (24)
11. Stuff the body.
12. Using the yarn leftover from the head, sew the body and head together at the open ends.

Legs (Make 2):

1. R1: ch 4, sc in 2nd ch through the hook, sc, 3 sc in next st, (working backwards) sc, 2 sc in last st.
2. R2: sc inc 1, sc, (sc inc 1) * 3, sc, (sc inc 1) * 2
3. R3: sc inc 1, sc, sc, (sc inc 1, sc) *3, sc, (sc inc 1, sc) *2
4. R4: sc in each st
5. R5: sc in 5 sts, (sc dec 1, sc in 2 sts) * 3, sc in 3 sts
6. R6: sc in 5 sts, (sc dec 1, sc in 1 st) * 3, sc in 3 sts
7. R7–8: sc in each st
8. FO leaving a long tail to sew.
9. Thrust the legs and attach them to the body.

Arms (Make 2):

1. R1: 6 sc in MR (6)
2. R2: sc inc in each st (12)
3. R3–9: sc in each st (12)
4. FO leaving a long tail to sew.
5. Thrust the arms and attach them to the body.

Tail:

1. R1: 6 sc in MR (6)
2. R2: (sc in 1 st, sc inc 1) * 3 (9)
3. R3–12: sc in each st (9)
4. FO leaving a long tail to sew.
5. Thrust the tail and attach it to the body.

Ears (Make 2):

1. R1: 6 sc in MR (6)
2. R2: sc inc in each st (12)
3. R3: (sc in 3 sts, sc inc 1) * 3 (15)
4. R4–5: sc in each st (15)
5. FO leaving a long tail to sew.
6. Attach to the head.

27.   Kimba the Lion

Your wild animal collection will not be complete without the king of the jungle. This lion pattern is simple and quick to make. The orange hair crocheted around the head gives him a majestic look.

What You Need:

- DK/ worsted yarn in the color of your choice
- Orange and white yarn
- 4 mm crochet hook
- A pair of 6 mm safety eyes
- Stuffing
- Embroidery needle to sew

Head:

1. R1: 6 sc in MR (6)
2. R2: sc inc in each st (12)
3. R3: (sc in 1 st, sc inc 1) * 6 (18)
4. R4:(sc in 2 sts, sc inc 1) *6 (24)
5. R5:(sc in 3 sts, sc inc 1) *6 (30)
6. R6:(sc in 4 sts, sc inc 1) *6 (36)
7. R7:(sc in 5 sts, sc inc 1) *6 (42)
8. R8: sc in each st (42)
9. R9:(sc in 6 sts, sc inc 1) *6 (48)
10. R10: sc in each st (48)
11. R11: (sc in 7 sts, sc inc 1) * 6 (54)
12. R12–17: sc in each st (54)
13. R18: (sc in 7 sts, sc dec 1) *6 (48)
14. R19: (sc in 6 sts, sc dec 1) *6 (42)
15. R20: (sc in 5 sts, sc dec 1) *6 (36)
16. R21: (sc in 4 sts, sc dec 1) * 6 (30)
17. R22: (sc in 3 sts, sc dec 1) * 6 (24)
18. Stuff the head.
19. FO leaving a long tail to sew.

Mouth:

1. Use white yarn
2. R1: 6 sc in MR (6)
3. R2: sc inc in each st (12)
4. R3: (sc in 1 st, sc inc 1) * 6 (18)
5. R4: (sc in 2 sts, sc inc 1) * 6 (24)
6. R5–6: sc in each st (24)
7. FO leaving a long tail to sew.
8. With orange yarn, sew a nose, and with black yarn sew the lips to the mouth. Stuff the mouth and attach the mouth to the head. Attach the safety eyes just above the mouth.

Body:

1. R1: 6 sc in MR (6)
2. R2: sc inc in each st (12)
3. R3: (sc in 1 st, sc inc 1) * 6 (18)
4. R4: (sc in 2 sts, sc inc 1) * 6 (24)
5. R5: (sc in 3 sts, sc inc 1) * 6 (30)
6. R6–10: sc in each st (30)
7. R11: (sci n 3 sts, sc dec 1) *6 (24)
8. R12–14: sc in each st (24)
9. Stuff the body.
10. Using the yarn left from the head, sew the body and head together at the open ends.

Legs (Make 2):

1. R1: ch 4, sc in 2nd ch through the hook, sc, 3 sc in next st, (working backwards) sc, 2 sc in last st.
2. R2: sc inc 1, sc, (sc inc 1) * 3, sc, (sc inc 1) * 2
3. R3: sc inc1, sc, sc, (sc inc 1, sc) *3, sc, (sc inc 1, sc) *2
4. R4: sc in each st
5. R5: sc in 5 sts, (sc dec 1, sc in 2 sts) * 3, sc in 3 sts

6. R6: sc in 5 sts, (sc dec 1, sc in 1 st) * 3, sc in 3 sts
7. R7–8: sc in each st
8. FO leaving a long tail to sew.
9. Thrust the legs and attach them to the body.

Arms (Make 2):

1. R1: 6 sc in MR (6)
2. R2: sc inc in each st (12)
3. R3–9: sc in each st (12)
4. FO leaving a long tail to sew.
5. Thrust the arms and attach them to the body.

Tail:

1. R1: Ch 15, sc in each ch.
2. FO leaving a long tail to sew.
3. Attach to the body.

Ears (Make 2):

1. R1: 6 sc in MR (6)
2. R2: sc inc in each st (12)
3. R3: (sc in 3 sts, sc inc 1) * 3 (15)
4. R4–5: sc in each st (15)
5. FO leaving a long tail to sew.
6. Attach to the head.
7. Using orange yarn, cut 4 5-inch strands.
8. Attach these to the tip of the tail using a knot.

Hair:

1. Use orange yarn.
2. R1: Ch 60, turn
3. R2: sc in next st, (hdc in next st, {dc, tr, dc} in next st, hdc in the next st, sl st in next st) * till the end.
4. FO leaving a long tail to sew.
5. Attach the hair around the head and secure it with straight stitches.

28.   Arlo the Baby Dinosaur

This lovable baby Arlo pattern will leave you swooning. It is a simple pattern that you can vary in length by using larger crochet hooks. Use any color yarn you like. Add some spikes to turn the dinosaur into a different dinosaur species. Have fun with this pattern and go wild with the variations that are possible.

What You Need:

- ➢ DK/ worsted yarn in the color of your choice
- ➢ Black yarn
- ➢ 4 mm crochet hook
- ➢ A pair of 6 mm safety eyes
- ➢ Stuffing
- ➢ Embroidery needle to sew

Head:

1. R1: 6 sc in MR (6)
2. R2: sc inc in each st (12)
3. R3–4: sc in each st (12)
4. R5: sc inc * 3, sc in 9 sts (15)
5. R6–7: sc in each st (15)
6. R8: sc in 6 sts, (sc in 1 st, sc dec 1) * 3 (12)
7. Attach safety eyes at R6
8. R9: (sc in 1 st, sc dec 1) * 4 (8)
9. Stuff the head
10. R10: (sc in 1 st, sc dec 1) * 2, sl st (6)
11. Tighten off, leaving a long tail to sew.

Neck:

1. R1: 6 sc in MR (6)
2. R2–7: sc in each st (6)
3. Stuff the neck.
4. Tighten off, leaving a long tail to sew.

5. Attach the neck to the head.
6. Using black yarn, sew a mouth on the head.

Body:

1. R1: 6 sc in MR (6)
2. R2: sc inc in each st (12)
3. R3: (sc in 1 st, sc inc 1) * 6 (18)
4. R4–10: sc in each st (18)
5. R11: (sc in 1 st, sc dec 1) * 6 (12)
6. Stuff the body.
7. R12: sc dec * 6 (6)
8. Tighten off leaving a long tail to sew.
9. Attach the body to the lower part of the neck.

Feet (Make 4):

1. R1: 6 sc in MR (6)
2. R2–7: sc in each st (6)
3. Stuff the neck.
4. Tighten off leaving a long tail to sew.

5. Attach the feet to the body.

Tail:

1. R1: 4 sc in MR (4)
2. R2: sc in each st (4)
3. R3: (sc in 1 st, sc inc 1) * 2 (6)
4. R4: (sc in 2 sts, sc inc 1) * 2 (8)
5. R5: sc in each st (8)
6. R6: (sc in 3 sts, sc inc 1) * 2 (10)
7. R7: sc in each st (10)
8. R8: (sc in 4 sts, sc inc 1) * 2 (12)
9. R9: sc in each st (12)
10. Stuff the tail.
11. Tighten off, leaving a long tail to sew.
12. Attach the tail to the body.

Adornments (Make 3):

1. R1: 6 sc in MR (6)
2. Tighten off, leaving a long tail to sew.
3. Attach the circles to the side of the body.

We now introduce some of the creatures of the wild that intrigue us. We are talking about the bugs and the bees! These stunning creatures are a dream to crochet. They can be used as accessories like keychains, showpieces, etc. So, crochet away these cute ones and build up your collection of The Incredibles.

29. Katy the Caterpillar

Isn't she a beauty? Katy, the caterpillar, is a colorful toy that you can easily crochet in no time. Use up any odd yarn that you have to create this beautiful toy. You can make her as long as you like by just adding additional body segments.

What You Need:

➢ DK/ worsted yarn in colors of your choice
➢ 3.5 mm crochet hook
➢ A pair of 6 mm safety eyes
➢ Stuffing
➢ Embroidery needle to sew

Body:

1. R1: 6 sc in MR (6)
2. R2: inc in each st (12)
3. R3: (sc 1, inc 1) *6 (18)
4. R4: (sc 2, inc 1) *6 (24)
5. R5: (sc 3, inc 1) *6 (30)
6. R6: (sc 4, inc 1) *6 (36)
7. R7: (sc 5, inc 1) *6 (42)
8. R8: (sc 6, inc 1) *6 (48)
9. R9–16: sc in each st (48)
10. R17: (sc 6, dec 1) *6 (42)
11. R18: (sc 5, dec 1) *6 (36)
12. R19: (sc 4, dec 1) *6 (30)
13. R20: (sc 3, dec 1) *6 (24)
14. R21: (sc 2, dec 1) *6 (18)
15. First body segment made. Stuff well. Now change color to create the next segment. Stuff after each segment is created.
16. Repeat R4–R21 four times.
17. R22: (sc 1, dec 1) *6 (12)
18. R23: dec * 6 (6)
19. Stuff the body. Fasten off and weave in the ends.

Head:

1. R1: 6 sc in MR (6)
2. R2: inc in each st (12)
3. R3: (sc 1, inc 1) *6 (18)
4. R4: (sc 2, inc 1) *6 (24)
5. R5: (sc 3, inc 1) *6 (30)
6. R6: (sc 4, inc 1) *6 (36)
7. R7: (sc 5, inc 1) *6 (42)
8. R8: (sc 6, inc 1) * (48)
9. R9: (sc 7, inc 1) *6 (54)
10. Attach the eyes at R4.
11. Sew a mouth with red yarn.
12. R10-17: sc in each st (54)
13. R18: (sc 7, dec 1) *6 (48)
14. R19: (sc 6, dec 1) *6 (42)
15. R20: (sc 5, dec 1) *6 (36)
16. R21: (sc 4, dec 1) *6 (30)
17. R22: (sc 3, dec 1) *6 (24)
18. R23: (sc 2, dec 1) *6 (18)
19. Stuff the head.
20. R24: (sc 1, dec 1) *6 (12)
21. R25: dec * 6 (6)
22. Fasten off and weave in the ends. Sew the head to the body.

Antennae (Make 2):

1. R1: 6 sc in MR (6)
2. R2: inc in each st (12)
3. R3: (sc 3, inc 1) * 3 (15)
4. R4–6: sc in each st (15)
5. R7: (sc 1, dec 1) * 6 (10)
6. R8–12: sc in each st (10)
7. FO leaving a long tail to sew. Sew the antennae on the head.

Feet (Make 10):

1. Ch 8, hdc in 3 nd ch from hook, hdc in remaining ch.
2. FO leaving a long tail to sew.
3. Sew two feet onto each of the body segments.

30.   Ollie the Owl

Here is an all-time favorite toy that kids and adults adore. We give you a tiny pattern that can be used for various things like ornaments, keychains, etc. So have fun with this pattern and choose bright and bold colors to give your owl the edge.

What You Need:

> - DK/ worsted yarn in the color of your choice
> - White and pink yarn
> - 3 mm crochet hook
> - A pair of black buttons
> - Stuffing
> - Embroidery needle to sew

Body:

1. Use yarn color of your choice (A)
2. R1: 6 sc in MR (6)
3. R2: inc in each st (12)
4. R3: (sc 1, inc 1) *6 (18)
5. R4: (sc 2, inc 1) *6 (24)
6. R5: (sc 3, inc 1) *6 (30)
7. R6: (sc 4, inc 1) *6 (36)
8. R7: (sc 5, inc 1) *6 (42)
9. R8: (sc 6, inc 1) *6 (48)
10. R9: (sc 7, inc 1) *6 (54)
11. R10−20: sc in each st (54)
12. R21: (sc 7, dec 1) *6 (48)
13. R22: sc in each st (48)
14. R23: (sc 6, dec 1) *6 (42)
15. R24: sc in each st (42)
16. R25: (sc 5, dec 1) *6 (36)
17. R26: sc in each st (36)
18. R27: (sc 4, dec 1) * 6 (30)
19. R28: sc in each st (30)
20. Stuff the body well.
21. Fold the body and sc across the top to close the gap.

Eyes (Make 2):

1. Use white yarn
2. R1: 6sc in MR (6)
3. R2: inc in each st (12)
4. R3: (sc 1, inc 1) * 6 (18)
5. FO leaving a long tail to sew.
6. Place the eyes on the body keeping a distance of 3 sts in between.
7. Place a black button in the center of each eye and sew the eyes in place.

Beak:

1. Use pink yarn
2. Ch4, sl st in 2 nd ch from hook, sc in the next 2 sts.
3. FO leaving a long tail to sew.
4. Sew the beak in place.

31.   Bitsy the Ladybug

Bitsy is a bright and eye-catching toy that you can crochet with ease. Bitsy is used as a pincushion here. You can choose to play with her or use her as a keychain too. So, the ideas are endless. Make a number of them and give them as a gift to your loved ones too.

What You Need:

- ➢ DK/ worsted yarn in red and black
- ➢ 4 mm crochet hook
- ➢ A pair of 3 mm safety eyes
- ➢ Wire antennae
- ➢ Stuffing
- ➢ Embroidery needle to sew

Body:

Top Half:

1. Use red yarn
2. R1: 6 sc in MR (6)
3. R2: sc inc in each st (12)
4. R3: (sc in 1 st, sc inc 1) * 6 (18)
5. R4: (sc in 2 sts, sc inc 1) *6 (24)
6. R5: (sc in 3sts, sc inc 1) *6 (30)
7. R6: (sc in 4 sts, sc inc 1) *6 (36)
8. R7: (sc in 5 sts, sc inc 1) *6 (42)
9. R8–16: sc in each st (42)
10. Fasten off.

Bottom Half:

1. Use black yarn.
2. R1: 6 sc in MR (6)
3. R2: sc inc in each st (12)
4. R3: (sc in 1 st, sc inc 1) * 6 (18)

5. R4: (sc in 2 sts, sc inc 1) * 6 (24)
6. R5: (sc in 3 sts, sc inc 1) * 6 (30)
7. R6: (sc in 4 sts, sc inc 1) * 6 (36)
8. R7: (sc in 5 sts, sc inc 1) * 6 (42)
9. R8: sc in each st (42)
10. Fasten off.
11. Sew the top and bottom half of the body together. Stuff as you go.

Head:

1. Use black yarn
2. R1: 6 sc in MR (6)
3. R2: sc inc in each st (12)
4. R3: (sc in 1 st, sc inc 1) * 6 (18)
5. R4: (sc in 2 sts, sc inc 1) * 6 (24)
6. R5-8: sc in each st (24)
7. R9: (sc in 2 sts, sc dec 1) *6 (18)
8. Stuff the head.
9. Tighten off, leaving a long tail to sew.
10. Attach the head to the body.
11. Using red yarn, sew a mouth to the head.
12. Using black yarn, sew a straight stitch in the center of the body.
13. Attach the wire antennae to the head.

Legs (Make 6):

1. Use black yarn
2. R1: 4 sc in MR (4)
3. R2–4: sc in each st (4)
4. Tighten off, leaving a long tail to sew.
5. Attach the legs to the body.

Dots (Make 6):

1. Use black yarn
2. R1: 6 sc in MR (6)
3. R2: sc inc in each st (12)
4. Tighten off, leaving a long tail to sew.
5. Attach the dots around the body and sew them in place.

32.   Abbie the Bee

Another buzzing companion you can crochet is Abbie, the Bee. She is waiting to zoom around in your garden. So, crochet this quick pattern and have fun. You can easily create many little bees in a short span of time. So, enjoy filling your garden with these cuties, or best yet, gift them to friends.

What You Need:

- ➤ DK/ worsted yarn in yellow and black
- ➤ White, black, and yellow yarn
- ➤ 2 mm crochet hook
- ➤ A pair of 3 mm safety eyes
- ➤ Stuffing
- ➤ Embroidery needle to sew

Body:

1. Use yellow yarn
2. R1: 6 sc in MR (6)
3. R2: sc inc in each st (12)
4. R3: (sc in 1 st, sc inc 1) * 6 (18)
5. R4: (sc in 2 sts, sc inc 1) *6 (24)
6. R5: (sc in 3 sts, sc inc 1) *6 (30)
7. R6: (sc in 4 sts, sc inc 1) *6 (36)
8. R7: (sc in 5 sts, sc inc 1) *6 (42)
9. R8–10: sc in each st (42)
10. CC black yarn
11. R11-–13: sc in each st (42)
12. CC yellow yarn
13. R14–17: sc in each st (42)
14. CC black yarn
15. R18–20: sc in each st (42)
16. CC yellow yarn

17. R21–22: sc in each st (42)
18. R23: (sc in 5 sts, sc dec 1) *6 (36)
19. R24: (sc in 4 sts, sc dec 1) *6 (30)
20. R25:(sc in 3 sts, sc dec 1) *6 (24)
21. R26: (sc in 2 sts, sc dec 1) *6 (18)
22. Stuff the body.
23. R27: (sc in 1 st, sc dec 1) *6 (12)
24. R28: dec in each st (6)
25. Fasten off and weave in the ends.
26. Fix safety eyes to the front of the body.

Antennae (Make 2):

1. Using black yarn, Ch 6 and fasten off.
2. Attach this to the top of the head.

Tail:

1. Use black yarn.
2. R1: 4 sc in MR (4)
3. R2–7: sc in each st (4)
4. R8: (sc in 1 st, sc inc) *2 (6)
5. Tighten off, leaving a long tail to sew.
6. Attach the tail to the body.

Legs (Make 6):

1. Use black yarn
2. R1: 4 sc in MR (4)
3. R2-4: sc in each st (4)
4. Tighten off, leaving a long tail to sew.
5. Attach the legs to the body.

Wings (Make 2):

1. Use white yarn
2. R1: 6 sc in MR (6)
3. R2: sc inc in each st (12)
4. R3: (sc in 1 st, sc inc 1) * 6 (18)
5. R4: sl st in 9 sts, (sc in 2 sts, sc inc 1) *3 (21)
6. Fasten off, leaving a long tail to sew.
7. Attach the wings to the top of the body.

33.   Berty the Bat

Berty the Bat may look scary but he is a cutie really. This is a pretty simple pattern to work with. Create Berty in various colors for a whole range of toys. Change the crochet hook size to have the same pattern in different sizes.

What You Need:

- ➢ DK/ worsted yarn in the color of your choice
- ➢ White and black yarn
- ➢ White felt
- ➢ 3 mm crochet hook
- ➢ A pair of 8 mm safety eyes
- ➢ Stuffing
- ➢ Embroidery needle to sew

Body:

1. Use yarn color of your choice
2. R1: 6 sc in MR (6)
3. R2: sc inc in each st (12)
4. R3: (sc in 1 st, sc inc 1) * 6 (18)
5. R4: (sc in 2 sts, sc inc 1) * 6 (24)
6. R5: (sc in 3 sts, sc inc 1) * 6 (30)
7. R6: (sc in 4 sts, sc inc 1) * 6 (36)
8. R7: (sc in 5 sts, sc inc 1) * 6 (42)
9. R8–13: sc in each st (42)
10. R14: (sc in 5 sts, sc dec 1) *6 (36)
11. R15: (sc in 4 sts, sc dec 1) *6 (30)
12. You can now attach the eyes between R12 and R13 with 6 sts in between. Using black yarn, sew a mouth on R14.
13. R16: (sc in 3 sts, sc dec 1) *6 (24)
14. R17: (sc in 2 sts, sc dec 1) *6 (18)

15. Stuff the body.
16. R18: (sc in 1 st, sc dec 1) *6 (12)

17. R19: dec in each st (6)
18. Fasten off and weave in the ends.

Ears (Make 2):

1. R1: 5 sc in MR (5)
2. R2: sc inc 1, (sc in 2 sts, sc inc 1) * 2 (8)
3. R3: (sc in 1 st, sc inc 1) * 4 (12)
4. R4: (sc in 2 sts, sc inc 1) * 4 (16)
5. R5: (sc in 3 sts, sc inc 1) * 4 (20)
6. R6:(sc in 3 sts, sc dec 1) *4 (16)
7. R7: (sc in 2 sts, sc dec 1) *4 (12)
8. Tighten off, leaving a long tail to sew.
9. Sew the ears to the top of the body.

Wings (Make 2):

1. R1: Ch12, turn
2. R2: (sl st, sc in 4 sts, sc dec, sl st) * 4, ch1, turn
3. R3: sc inc, sc inc, sc in 8 sts, ch1, turn
4. R4: sc in 3 sts, sc dec, sc in 5 sts, ch1, turn
5. R5: sc in 3 sts, sc dec, sc in 4 sts, ch1, turn
6. R6: sl st in 5 sts, ch2, sl st
7. Fasten off, leaving a long tail to sew.
8. Attach the wings between R10 and R14.
9. You can cut out tiny teeth from the white felt and glue them onto the mouth.

34.   Bubba Blue Bird

What You Need:

- Cotton yarn
- Crochet needle 5 mm
- Stuff fiber
- Safety eyes
- Sewing needle
- Scissors

Head:

1. Begin with the magic ring.
2. R1: 6 Sc into the magic ring. Close the magic ring with a SL St= (6 Sts).

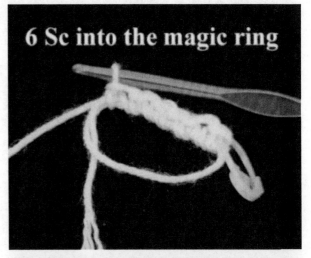

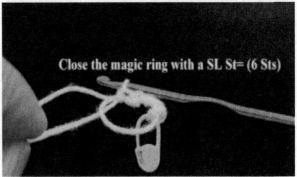

NOTE: Don't forget to put the stitch marker in the first stitch of each round.

3. Rnd 2: 1 INC in each stitch = (12 Sts).

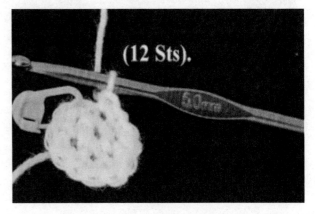

4. Rnd 3: (1 Sc, 1 INC in the next stitch) repeat until the end of the round = (18 Sts).

(18 Sts).

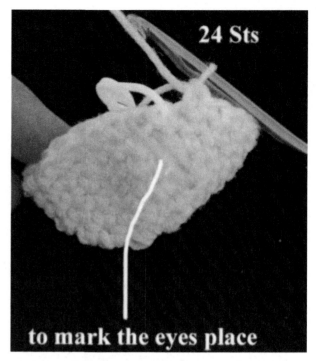

24 Sts

to mark the eyes place

5. Rnd 4: (2 Sc, 1 INC in the next stitch) repeat until the end of the round = (24 Sts).

7. Rnd 8: (3 Sc, 1 INC in the next stitch) repeat until the end of the round = (30 Sts).

(24 Sts).

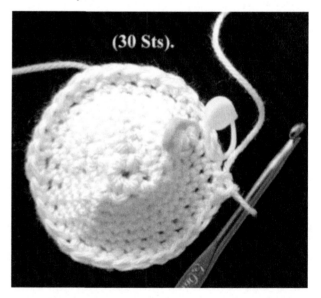

(30 Sts).

6. Rnd 5 to Rnd 7: 1 Sc around for 3 rounds= (24 Sts).

8. Rnd 9 to Rnd 12: 1 Sc around for 4 rounds= (30 Sts).

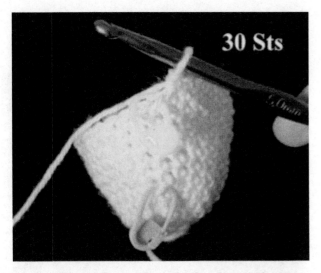

30 Sts

9. Then, change the color by slip stitch. Cut the first yarn and start the body pattern.

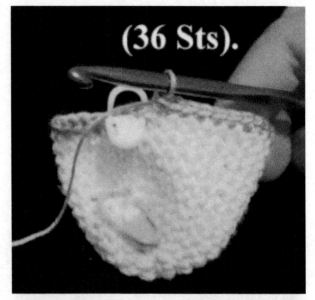

(36 Sts).

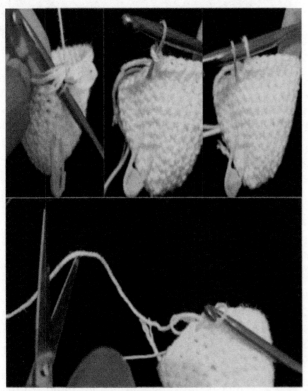

10. Rnd 13: (4 Sc, 1 INC in the next stitch) repeat until the end of the round = (36 Sts).

11. Rnd 14 to Rnd 27: 1 Sc around for 14 rounds= (36 Sts).
12. Rnd 28: (4 Sc, 1 Dec by 2 St Tog from the front loop) repeat until the end of the round = (30 Sts).

13. Then, put the safety eyes on at round 6 with 5 stitches between them. Use the orange color and purl the beak with the sewing needle.

14. Rnd 29: (3 Sc, 1 Dec by 2 St Tog from the front loop) repeat until the end of the round = (24 Sts).
15. Rnd 30: (2 Sc, 1 Dec by 2 St Tog from the front loop) repeat until the end of the round = (18 Sts).
16. Rnd 31: (1 Sc, 1 Dec by 2 St Tog from the front loop) repeat until the end of the round = (12 Sts).
17. Then, stuff the bird with fiber.

18. Rnd 32: 6 Dec by 2 St Tog from the front loop = (6 Sts).
19. Slip stitch and Ch 1, then cut the yarn.

Wings (Make 4):

1. Begin with the magic ring.
2. R1: 6 Sc into the magic ring. Close the magic ring with a SL St= (6 Sts).

NOTE: Don't forget to put the stitch marker in the first stitch of each round

3. Rnd 2: 1 INC in each stitch = (12 Sts).
4. Rnd 3: (1 Sc, 1 INC in the next stitch) repeat until the end of the round = (18 Sts).
5. Rnd 4: (2 Sc, 1 INC in the next stitch) repeat until the end of the round = (24 Sts).
6. Rnd 5: (3 Sc, 1 INC in the next stitch) repeat until the end of the round = (30 Sts).
7. Rnd 6: (4 Sc, 1 INC in the next stitch) repeat until the end of the round = (36 Sts).
8. Slip stitch and Ch1, then cut the yarn.

Tail:

1. Begin with the magic ring.
2. R1: 6 Sc into the magic ring. Close the magic ring with a SL St= (6 Sts).

NOTE: Don't forget to put the stitch marker in the first stitch of each round.

3. Rnd 2: (1 Sc, 1 INC in the next stitch) repeat until the end of the round = (9 Sts).

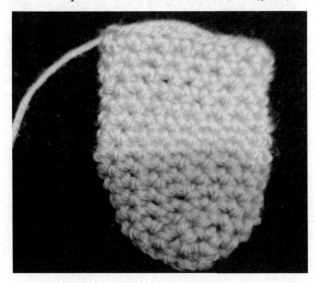

4. Rnd 3 to Rnd 4: 1 Sc around for 2 rounds= (9 Sts).
5. Rnd 5: (2 Sc, 1 INC in the next stitch) repeat until the end of the round = (12 Sts).

6. Rnd 6 to Rnd 7: 1 Sc around for 2 rounds= (12 Sts).
7. Rnd 8: (3 Sc, 1 INC in the next stitch) repeat until the end of the round = (15 Sts).
8. Rnd 9 to Rnd 18: 1 Sc around for 10 rounds= (15 Sts).
9. Cut the yarn and leave a long tail, then stuff the tail with fiber.

Feet:

1. Begin with the magic ring.
2. Do 3 Sc into the magic ring, then turn your work.
3. Ch4, then do 3 Sc on the chain from chain 2.
4. Sl St into the first stitch.

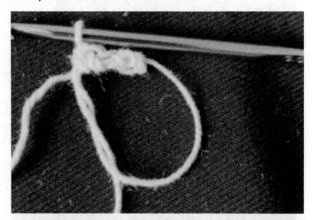

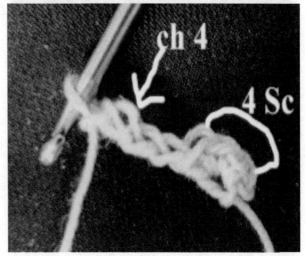

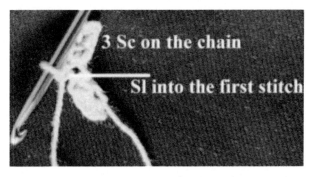

5. Ch4, then do 3 Sc on the chain from chain 2.
6. Sl St into the second stitch.

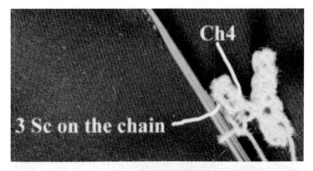

7. Ch4. Then do 3 Sc on the chain from chain 2.
8. Sl St into the last stitch, Ch1, cut the yarn, and fasten off.

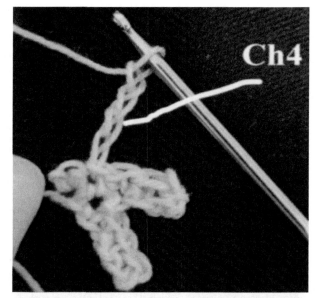

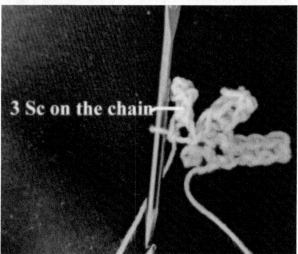

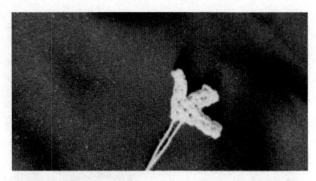

Assembly:

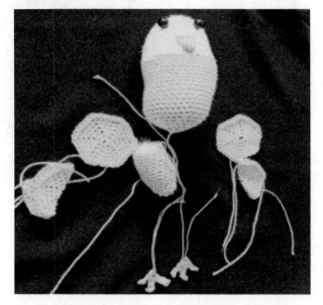

1. With the sewing needle, assemble all the bird parts. Decorate it with black yarn, placing the yarn randomly.

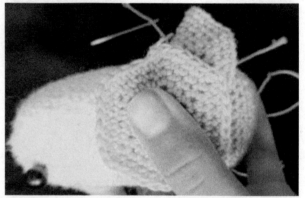

put the wing this way
wipe one and cover alittle
part of it
with the other

35. Mr. Thumper

Mr. Thumper is 22 inches in length. You may choose to make it using a single color or multi-colored like Mr. Thumper here. Bunnies are one of the trendiest animals to crochet for amigurumi crocheters. The cute face, the long ears, and the softail make anyone fall in love with them!

What You Need:

- ➤ 6 mm crochet hook
- ➤ Cotton flannel fabric in a color of your choice
- ➤ Two 15 mm safety eyes
- ➤ Large pompom maker (9 cm diameter)
- ➤ Colored tapestry wool (color of your choice)
- ➤ Red ribbon for the bowtie
- ➤ Stuffing
- ➤ Stitch markers
- ➤ Sewing thread
- ➤ Sewing needle
- ➤ Tapestry needle

Head:

1. R1: 6 sc in MR (6)
2. R2: inc *6 (12)
3. R3: (inc, sc in next st) *6 (18)
4. R4: (inc, sc in next 2 st) *6 (24)
5. R5: (inc, sc in next 3 st) *6 (30)
6. R6: (inc, sc in next 4 st) *6 (36)
7. R7: (inc, sc in next 5 st) *6 (42)
8. R8: (inc, sc in next 6 st) *6 (48)
9. R9: (inc, sc in next 7 st) *6 (54)
10. R10: (inc, sc in next 8 st) *6 (60)
11. R11 – 18 (8 rounds): sc in each st around (60)
12. R19: (dec, sc in next 8 st) *6 (54)
13. R20: (dec, sc in next 7 st) *6 (48)
14. R21: (dec, sc in next 6 st) *6 (42)
15. Put the safety eyes between rounds 16 and 17 approx. 16 st apart.
16. Start thrusting the head and continue as you go.
17. R22: (dec, sc in next 5 st) *6 (36)
18. R23: (dec, sc in next 4 st) *6 (30)
19. R24: (dec, sc in next 3 st) *6 (24)
20. Fasten off and weave in the ends.
21. Use pink thread to sew the nose between rounds 15 and 17 making long stitches to create a pink triangle.
22. Use black thread to sew the mouth under the nose between rounds 18 and 20.

Ears (Make 2):

1. R1: start 6 sc in MR (6)
2. R2: (inc, sc in next 2 st) *2 (8)
3. R3: (inc, sc in next 3 st) *2 (10)
4. R4: (inc, sc in next 4 st) *2 (12)
5. R5: (inc, sc in next 5 st) *2 [14]
6. R6: (inc, sc in next 6 st) *2 [16]
7. R7–21 (15 rounds): sc in each st around (16)
8. R22: dec, sc in next 14 st (15)
9. R23: sc in each st around (15)
10. R24: dec, sc in next 13 st (14)
11. R25: sc in each st around (14)
12. R26: dec, sc in next 12 st (13)
13. R27: sc in each st around (13)
14. R28: dec, sc in next 11 st (12)
15. R29: sc in each st around (12)
16. R30: dec, sc in next 10 st (11)
17. R31: sc in each st around (11)
18. R32: dec, sc in next 9 st (10)
19. R33: sc in each st around (10)

20. Do not thrust.
21. Tighten off, leaving a long tail for sewing the ears between rounds 6 and 8 of the head.

Body:

1. R1: start 6 sc in MR (6)
2. R2: inc *6 (12)
3. R3: (inc, sc in next st) *6 (18)
4. R4: (inc, sc in next 2 st) *6 (24)
5. R5: (inc, sc in next 3 st) *6 (30)
6. R6: (inc, sc in next 4 st) *6 (36)
7. R7: (inc, sc in next 5 st) *6 (42)
8. R8: (inc, sc in next 6 st) *6 (48)
9. R9–13: sc in each st around (48)
10. R14: (dec, sc in next 6 st) *6 (42)
11. R15–17: sc in each st around (42)
12. R18: (dec, sc in next 5 st) *6 (36)
13. R19–21: sc in each st around (36)
14. R22: (dec, sc in next 4 st) *6 (30)
15. R23–25: sc in each st around (30)
16. R26: (dec, sc in next 3 st) *6 (24)
17. Stuff the body.
18. Tighten off, leaving a long tail for sewing the body to the head.

Arms (Make 2):

1. R1: start 6 sc in MR (6)
2. R2: inc *6 (12)
3. R3–9: sc in each st around (12)
4. R10: dec, sc in next 10 st (11)
5. R11–12: sc in each st around (11)
6. R13: dec, sc in next 9 st (10)
7.

7. R14–19: sc in each st around (10)
8. Stuff lightly.
9. Fasten off. Parting a long tail to sew the arms to the trunk part.

Legs (Make 2):

1. R1: start 6 sc in MR (6)
2. R2: inc *6 (12)
3. R3: (inc, sc in next st) *6 (18)
4. R4: (inc, sc in next 2 st) *6 (24)
5. R5–9: sc in each st around (24)
6. R10: (dec, sc in next 6 st) *3 (21)
7. R11: sc in each st around (21)
8. R12: (dec, sc in next 5 st) *3 (18)
9. R13–15: sc in each st around (18)
10. R16: (dec, sc in next 4 st) *3 (15)
11. R17–19: sc in each st around (15)
12. R20: (dec, sc in next 3 st) *3 times (12)
13. R21–23: sc in each st around (12)
14. R24: (dec, sc in next 2 st) *3 times (9)
15. R25–27: sc in each st around (9)
16. Stuff lightly.
17. Fasten off. Parting a long tail to sew the legs to the body.

Tail:

1. Using a pompom maker, produce a 3.5-inch-diameter pompom.
2. To thread the pompom around the center, cut a long tail of yarn. Sew the pompom to the rear of the body using the same tail.
3. To add a bowtie, just make one out of red ribbon or any other color you choose.

36. Mr. Peck the Rooster

Isn't Mr. Peck so funny-looking and adorable? This may look like a complicated pattern, but if you closely follow the instructions, you will do a great job in creating this special character. You may also crochet another rooster and give it a name yourself!

What You Need:

- DK/ worsted yarn in colors (yellow, orange, red, brown, and white)
- 1.5 mm hook
- Stuffing
- Metal wire with a diameter of 0.9–1.0 mm
- Adhesive tape
- A pair of 10 mm safety eyes,
- A pair of artificial eyelashes

Head:

1. Use orange.
2. R1: 6 sc in MR
3. R2: 6 inc (12)
4. R3: (1 sc, inc) *6 (18)
5. R4: (2 sc, inc) *6 (24)
6. R5: (3 sc, inc) *6 (30)
7. R6: (4 sc, inc) *6 (36)
8. R7–12: 36 sc
9. R13: 6 sc, 6 inc, 12 sc, 6 inc, 6 sc (48)
10. R14: 6 sc, (1 sc, inc) *6, 12 sc, (inc, 1 sc) *6, 6 sc (60)
11. R15–20: 60 sc
12. R21: 60 sc,1 sc to move the beginning.
13. R22: 6 sc, (1 sc, dec) *6, 12 sc, (dec, 1sc) *6, 6 sc (48)
14. R23: 6 sc, 6 dec, 12 sc, 6 dec, 6 sc (36)
15. R24: (4 sc, dec) *6 times (30)

16. R25: (3 sc, dec) *6 times (24)
17. R26: (2 sc, dec) *6 times (18)
18. R27: 18 sc
19. Stuff well.
20. Fasten off and weave in the ends.

Beak:

Upper:

1. Use yellow.
2. R1: 3 sc in MR
3. R2: 3 inc (6)
4. R3: (1 sc, inc) *3 (9)
5. R4: 9 sc
6. R5: (2 sc, inc) *3 (12)
7. R6: 12 sc
8. R7: (3 sc, inc) *3 (15)
9. R8: (4 sc, inc) *3 (18)
10. R9: (2 sc, inc) *6 (24)
11. R10: (3 sc, inc) *6 (30)
12. R11: (4 sc, inc) *6 (36)
13. R12: (5 sc, inc) *6 (42)
14. R13: (6 sc, inc) *6 (48)
15. R14–16: 48 sc,
16. Finish and cut off the yarn.

Lower:

1. Use yellow.
2. R1: 3 sc in MR
3. R2: 3 inc *6)
4. R3: (1 sc, inc) *3 (9)
5. R4: 9 sc
6. R5: (2 sc, inc) *3 (12)
7. R6: 12 sc
8. R7: (3 sc, inc) *3 (15)
9. R8: (4 sc, inc) *3 (18)
10. R9: (2 sc, inc) *6 (24)
11. R10: (3 sc, inc) *6 (30)
12. R11: (4 sc, inc) *6 (36)
13. R12: (5 sc, inc) *6 (42)
14. R13: (6 sc, inc) *6 (48)
15. R14-16: 48 sc.
16. Finish, cut off the yarn.

Legs: Use brown.

Big toe (Make 2):

1. R1: 6 sc in MR
2. R2: 6 inc (12)
3. R3–4: 12 sc
4. R5: (1 sc, dec) *4 (8)
5. R6: (2 sc, dec) * 2 (6)
6. R7–12: 6 sc
7. Finish by cutting off the yarn and stuffing the toes.

Toe (Make 2):

1. R1: 6 sc in MR
2. R2: 6 inc (12)
3. R3–4: 12 sc
4. R5: (1 sc, dec) *4 (8)
5. R6: (2 sc, dec) *2 (6)
6. R7–11: 6 sc
7. For the last toe: Do not cut the yarn, thrust the toe. Collect the toes in a foot.

Foot:

1. R1: 3 sc on the 1st toe, 3 sc on the big toe, 6 sc on the 2nd toe, 3 sc on the big toe, 3 sc on the 1st toe 18 sc
2. R2–3: 18 sc
3. R4: (1 sc, dec) *6 (12)
4. R5: 2 sc, 3 ch, skip 3 sc, 7 sc (12)
5. R6: 2 sc, 3 sc in chains, 7 sc (12)
6. R7 rnd: 6 dec (6)
7. R8–9: 6 sc
8. R10: (1 sc, inc) *3 (9)
9. R11: 9 sc
10. R12: (1 sc, dec) *3 (6)
11. Finish by cutting off the yarn and closing the hole using a needle.

Leg:

1. 8 sc about the hole in the center of the foot.
2. R1–7: 8 sc
3. R8: (2 sc, dec) *2 (6)
4. R9–14: 6 sc.
5. Use orange.
6. R15: 6 inc (12)
7. R16: 12 sc
8. R17: (1 sc, inc) *6 (18)

9. R18–19: 18 sc
10. R20: (2 sc, inc) *6 (24)
11. R21: 24 sc
12. Tighten off and leave a long tail to sew other parts.

Wings: Use orange

The first feather (Make 2):

1. R1: 6 sc in MR
2. R2: 6 inc (12)
3. R3–5: 12 sc
4. R6: (1 sc, dec) *4 (8)
5. R7–10: 8 sc

The second feather (Make 2):

1. R1: 6 sc in MR
2. R2: 6 inc (12)
3. R3–5: 12 sc
4. R6: (1 sc, dec) *4 (8)
5. R7–12: 8 sc

The third feather (Make 2):

1. R1: 6 sc in MR
2. R2: 6 inc (12)
3. R3–5: 12 sc
4. R6 rnd (1 sc, dec) *4 (8)
5. R7–14: 8 sc

The fourth feather (Make 2):

1. R1: 6 sc in MR
2. R2: 6 inc (12)
3. R3–5: 12 sc
4. R6: (1 sc, dec) *4 (8)
5. R7–16: 8 sc
6. Keep the yarn and don't stop the feathers.
7. Attach feathers without replacing your row marker.
8. R17: 4 sc along the fourth feather, 8 sc along the third, 4 along the fourth, 16 sc
9. R18: 16 sc
10. R19: 8 sc, apply the second feather, make 8 sc along the second feather, 8 sc (24)
11. R20: 24 sc
12. R21: 12 sc, 8 sc along the first feather, 12 sc (32)
13. R22: 32 sc
14. R23: 8 sc, dec, 12 sc, dec, 8 sc (30)

15. R24: 7 sc, dec, 12 sc, dec, 7 sc (28)
16. R25: 6 sc, dec, 12 sc, dec, 6 sc (26)
17. R26: 5 sc, dec, 12 sc, dec, 5 sc (24)
18. R27: 4 sc, dec, 12 sc, dec, 4 sc (22)
19. R28: 3 sc, dec, 12 sc, dec, 3 sc (20)
20. R29: 2 sc, dec, 12 sc, dec, 2 sc (18)
21. R30: 1 sc, dec, 12 sc, dec, 1 sc (16)
22. R31: dec, 12, dec (14)
23. R32: dec, 10, dec (12)
24. R33–36: 12 sc
25. Finish. Leave a long tail to sew other parts.
26. Install a wire in the longest feather.

Body:

1. R1: 6 sc
2. R2: 6 inc (12)
3. R3: (1 sc, inc) *6 (18)
4. R4: (2 sc, inc) *6 (24)
5. R5: (3 sc, inc) *6 (30)
6. R6: (4 sc, inc) * 6 (36)
7. R7: (5 sc, inc) *6 (42)
8. R8: (6 sc, inc) *6 (48)
9. R9: (7 sc, inc) *6 (54)
10. R10: 1 ch, skip 1st, 7sc, inc, 8sc, inc, 3sc, 1ch, skip 1st, 4 sc, inc, (8 sc, inc) *3 (60)
11. R11: (9 sc, inc) *6 (66)
12. Make 1sc in the chains of the prior round.
13. R12: (10 sc, inc) *6 (72)
14. R13: (11 sc, inc) *6 (78)
15. R14-22: 78 sc
16. R23: 3 sc, (2 sc, dec) * 6, 51 sc (72)
17. R24: 3 sc, (1 sc, dec) *6, 51 sc (66)—this is where tail goes.
18. R25–27: 66 sc.
19. Install the leg wireframes, twist and separate.
20. R28: (9 sc, dec) *6 (60)
21. R29: (8 sc, dec) *6 (54)
22. R30: (7 sc, dec) * 6 (48)
23. R31: (6 sc, dec) *6 (42)
24. R32: (5 sc, dec) * 6 (36)
25. R33: (4 sc, dec) *6 (30)
26. Install the wing frames at the R27. Attach to the spine.
27. R34: (3 sc, dec) *6 (24)
28. R35: 24 sc
29. R36: (2 sc, dec) *6 (18)
30. R37-39: 18 sc
31. R40: (1 sc, dec) *6 (12)
32. R41–51: 12 sc
33. R52: (1 sc, inc) *6 (18)
34. Sew the wings.
35. Install the spine frame in the head.
36. Sew the head.
37. Sew the legs to the body.
38. Tail feathers (Make 3)
39. R1: 6 sc in MR
40. R2: 6 inc (12)
41. R3: (2 sc, inc) *4 (16)
42. R4-6: 16 sc
43. R7: (2 sc, dec) *4 (12)
44. R8-10: 12 sc
45. R11: (dec, 4 sc) *2 (10)
46. R12–14: 10 sc
47. R15: (dec, 3 sc) *2 (8)
48. R16-18: 8 sc
49. R19: (dec, 2 sc) * 2 (6)
50. R20–22: 6 sc
51. Connect all feathers using orange yarn.
52. R1: 3 sc along the first feather, 3 sc along the second, 6 sc along the third, 3 sc along the second,3 sc along the first, 18 sc
53. R2: 18 sc
54. R3: (1 sc, dec) *6 (12)
55. R4: (1 sc, inc) *6 (18)
56. R5: (2 sc, inc) * 6 (24)
57. R6: 24 sc
58. Finish and leave a long tail.

Cockscomb:

First part:

1. R1: 6 sc in MR
2. R2: 6 inc (12)
3. R3: (1 sc, inc) *6 (18)
4. R4–6: 18 sc
5. R7: (1 sc, dec) *6 (12)
6. R8-10: 12 sc
7. R11: (dec, 4 sc) * 2 (10)
8. R12–15: 10 sc
9. R16: (dec, 3 sc) * 2 (8)
10. R17–19: 8 sc

Second part:

1. R1: 6 sc in MR

2. R2: 6 inc (12)
3. R3: (1 sc, inc) *6 (18)
4. R4–6: 18 sc
5. R7: (1 sc, dec) * 6 (12)
6. R8–10: 12 sc
7. R11: (dec, 4 sc) * 2 (10)
8. R12–15: 10 sc
9. R16: (dec, 3 sc) *2 (8)
10. R17: 8 sc

Third part:

1. R1: 6 sc in MR
2. R2: 6 inc (12)
3. R3: (2 sc, inc) * 4 (16)
4. R4–6: 16 sc
5. R7: (2 sc, dec) *4 (12)
6. R8–9: 12 sc
7. R10: (dec, 4 sc) * 2 (10)
8. R11–13: 10 sc
9. R14: (dec, 3 sc) * 2 (8)
10. Connect all parts.
11. R15: 4 sc for the small part, 4 sc for the middle part, 8 sc for the big part, 4 sc for the middle part, 4 sc for the small part (24)
12. R16: 24 sc

37.   Majestic Unicorn

13. Attach to the head.

Beard (Make 2):

1. R1: 6 sc in MR
2. R2: 6 inc (12)
3. R3: (1 sc, inc) *6 (18)
4. R4–5: 18 sc
5. R6: (1 sc, dec) *6 (12)
6. R7–9: 12 sc
7. R10: 6 dec (6)
8. R11–12: 6 sc
9. Connect both beads using 3 sc.
10. Join the beak.

Eyes (Make 2):

1. Use white.
2. R1: 6 sc in MR (6)
3. R2: inc *6 (12)
4. R3: (1sc, inc) *6 (18)
5. R4: 18 sc (18)
6. R5: (1sc, dec) *6 (12)
7. Stuff lightly.
8. Install the eyes between the R2–3.
9. R6: dec *6 (6)
10. Join to the head.
11. Add eyelashes.

Wgat You Need:

➢ Cotton yarn
➢ Crochet needle 3.5 mm
➢ Fiberfill
➢ Safety eyes
➢ Sewing needle
➢ Embroidery yarn
➢ A little piece of cardboard, around the size of a playing card

5. R2: (1 Sc, INC in next St) repeat 3 times = (9 Sts).

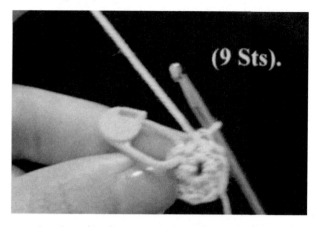

6. R3: (Sc in next 2 Sts, INC in next St) repeat 3 times = (12 Sts).

7. R4: Sc in each St = (12 Sts).
8. Change to the light color by Sl St into the first stitch.

Legs (Make 4):

1. Start with the darker color.
2. Begin with the magic ring.
3. R1: 6 Sc into the magic ring. Put the stitch marker on the first stitch.
4. Tighten the magic ring.

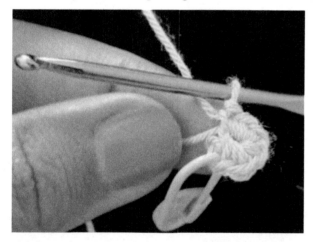

NOTE: In each round, first remove the stitch marker, then do the first stitch and put the stitch marker on that first stitch to mark the beginning of the round.

We will continue working in a spiral.

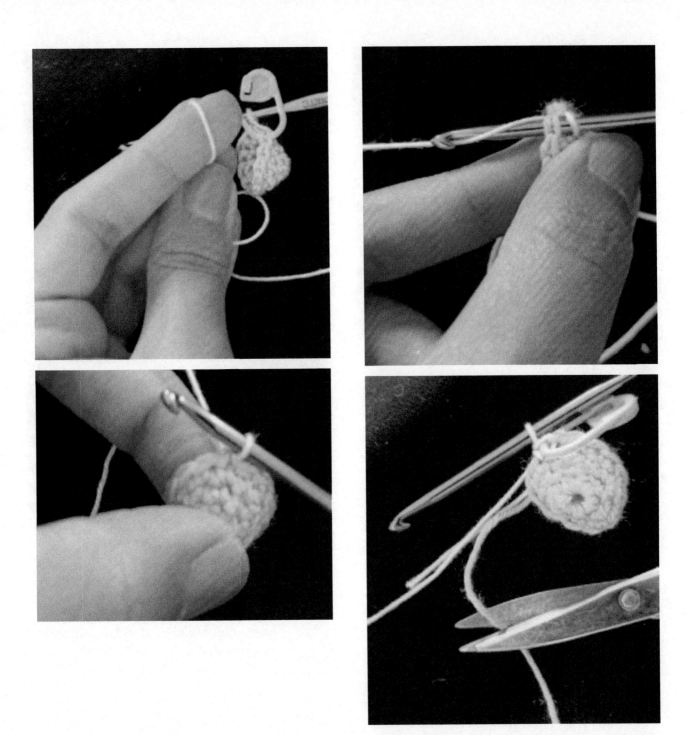

9. Rnd 5 to Rnd 10: Sc in each St = (12 Sts).
10. Leave the working yarn attached to the last leg.

11. Stuff each leg with a suitable amount of fiber.

12. Sew the legs together by sewing 3 stitches on each side of the legs. Use the same light color thread. Also, sew the middle hole closed with the remaining tail.

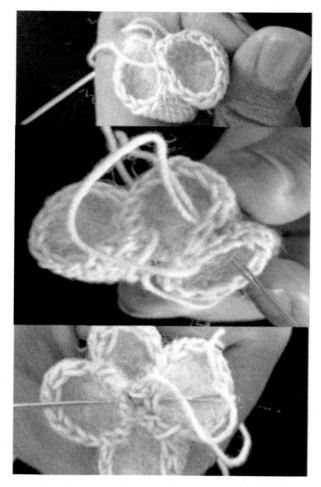

13. After you have attached the four legs together, you will have 24 Sts in total.

Body and Neck:

1. Start making the next round.

2. Expend a stitch marker to mark the beginning of this round and consider this round as Rnd 1: Sc in each St (24).

9. R14: (Sc in next 9 Sts, Dec by 2 St Tog from the front loop 3 times, Sc in next 9 St) = (21 Sts).
10. R15: (Sc in next 8 Sts, Dec by 2 St Tog from the front loop 3 times, Sc in next 7 St) = (18 Sts).
11. R16: (Sc in next 7 Sts, Dec by 2 St Tog from the front loop 3 times, Sc in next 5 St) = (15 Sts).
12. Rnd 17 to Rnd 20: Sc in each St = (15 Sts).
13. Fasten off by slip stitch chain 1 and cut the yarn.

3. R2: (Sc in next 3 Sts, INC in next St) repeat 6 times = (30 Sts).
4. Rnd 3: (Sc in next 4 Sts, INC in next St) repeat 6 times = (36 Sts).
5. Rnd 4 to Rnd 11: Sc in each St = (36 Sts).
6. Rnd 12: (Sc in next 12 Sts, Dec by 2 St Tog from the front loop 6 times, Sc in next 12 Sts) = (30 Sts).
7. Rnd 13: (Sc in next 9 Sts, Dec by 2 St Tog from the front loop 6 times, Sc in the next 9 Sts) = (24 Sts).

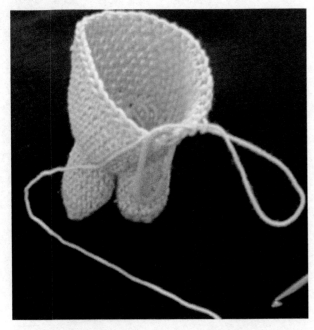

14. Stuff it with fiber, but not completely, just enough to give it some shape.

Head:

15. Use the lighter color thread.
16. R1: Begin with a magic ring and do 6 Sc into it. Put the stitch marker on the first stitch.
17. Tighten the magic ring.

NOTE: In each round, first remove the stitch marker, then do the first stitch and put the stitch marker on it to mark the beginning of the round.

8. Stuff the body with a suitable amount of fiber.

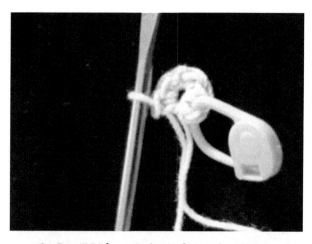

18. R2: INC by 2 Sc in each St= (12 Sts).

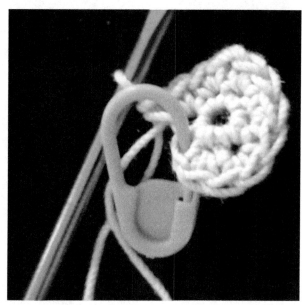

19. R3: (1 Sc, INC in next St) repeat 6 times = (18 Sts).

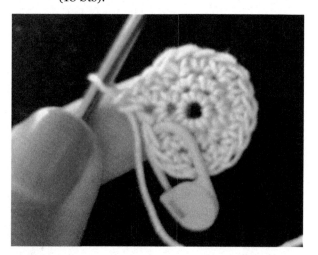

20. Rnd 4 to Rnd 6: Sc in each St = (18 Sts).
21. Rnd 7: (1 Sc, INC in next St) repeat 6 times, Sc in next 6 Sts = (24 sts).
22. Rnd 8: (1 Sc, INC in next St) repeat 6 times, Sc in next 12 Sts = (30 Sts).
23. Rnd 9 to Rnd 15: Sc in each St = (30 Sts).
24. Then attach the eyes in Rnd 8 and count 14 stitches between them.
25. Stuff the head with a suitable amount of fiber.
26. R16: (Sc in next 3 Sts, Dec by 2 St Tog from the front loop) repeat 6 times = (24 sts).
27. R17: (Sc in next 2 Sts, Dec by 2 St Tog from the front loop) repeat 6 times = (18 sts).
28. R18: (Sc in next St, Dec by 2 St Tog from the front loop) repeat 6 times = (12 sts).
29. Stuff the head a little bit.
30. Rnd 19: DEC by 2 St Tog from the front loop 6 times = (6 Sts).
31. Fasten off by slip stitch, chain 1, then cut the yarn and leave a long tail yarn.

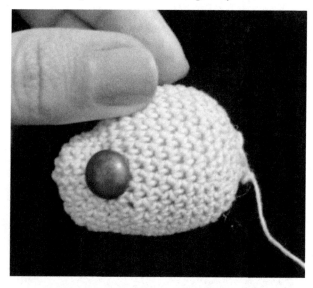

32. Place the head onto the neck in a suitable position and sew them together by the long tail yarn using the sewing needle.

Ears (Make 2):

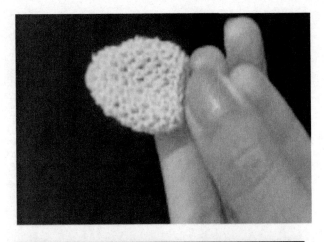

1. Make 2 ears with the same light color as the head.
2. Rnd 1: Begin with a magic ring and do 6 Sc into it.
3. Rnd 2: (1 Sc, INC in next St) repeat 3 times = (9 Sts).
4. Rnd 3: Sc in each St = (9 Sts).
5. R4: (Sc in the next 2 Sts, INC in next St) repeat 3 times = (12 sts).
6. R5: (Sc in the next 3 Sts, INC in next St) repeat 3 times = (15 sts).
7. Rnd 6 to Rnd 8: Sc in each St = (15 Sts).
8. R9: (Sc in the next 3 Sts, Dec by 2 St Tog from the front loop) repeat 3 times = (12 sts).
9. Rnd 10: Sc in each St = (12 Sts).
10. Fasten off by slip stitch, chain one, then cut the yarn and leave a long tail of yarn.
11. Place them onto both sides of the head.

Horn:

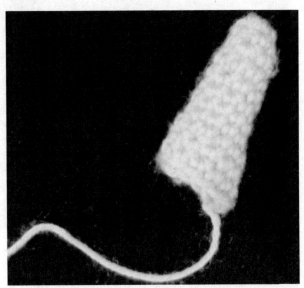

With the dark color thread:

1. Rnd 1: Begin with a magic ring and do 6 Sc into it.
2. Rnd 2: Sc in each St = (6 Sts).
3. Rnd 3: (Sc in next 2 Sts, INC in next St) repeat 2 times = (8 sts).
4. Rnd 4: Sc in each St = (8 Sts).
5. Rnd 5: (Sc in next 3 Sts, INC in next St) repeat 2 times = (10 sts).
6. Rnd 6: Sc in each St = (10 Sts).

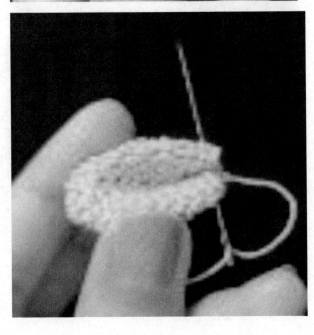

113

7. Rnd 7: (Sc in next 4 Sts, INC in next St) repeat 2 times = (12 sts).
8. Rnd 8 to Rnd 10: Sc in each St = (12 Sts).
9. Fasten off by slip stitch, chain one, then cut the yarn and leave a long tail of yarn.
10. Place it onto the head.

Mane and Tail:

1. Wrap about 10cm (about 4 inches) of yarn around a piece of cardboard roughly 7 times.

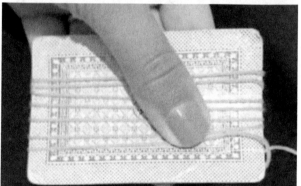

2. Cut the loops on one end of the cardboard.

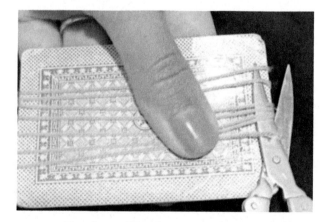

3. Use the embroidery yarn to sew the hair yarn onto the head in a suitable place. Also, sew some of the hair yarn onto the back to make the tail.

4. Sew the eyebrows and the mouth by using the embroidery yarn.

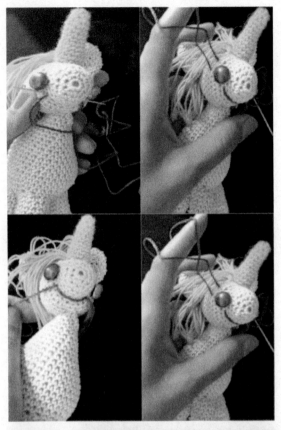

Crocheting is a fun craft that you have to try. The learning journey is not long nor a hard one and it will only take a few attempts until you get the hang of it. Once you start, you will find yourself willing and keen in taking on bigger and more tricky projects.

The two main components you will need for crochet are: a hook and yarn. The choice of the hook is up to you, as long as you find it easy to use. The yarn type is totally dependent on your taste. Many people tend to use wool, while others prefer cotton or acrylics. Scissors and stitch markers are tools which make crocheting easier, although not absolutely necessary. For beginners, I would recommend using a hook size between E-H. And remember going too big will make your work harder, it's better to start out with something easy when you're starting out!

Crocheting is a fantastic way to make one-of-a-kind, personalized gifts, as well as beautiful decorations for your home or clothing. There is no better feeling than making something and having it appreciated by others!

Crocheting is ever-increasing in popularity for a wide range of reasons!

Not only is it fun to create your own clothing, home decor, toys, and a brilliant style to show your creativity but it is also relaxing, entertaining and often it creates a strong bond with friends or family if you decide to collaborate on a project.

Before you get started on your projects, remember, that it is important not to cut the strand flush with the knot after sewing. Because of repetitive use and washing, the cut knot would end up falling apart and could ruin your piece.

For this not to happen, you must leave enough thread to hide it and finish off the project perfectly.

Your journey in understanding Crochet is not a long or difficult one, as it only takes a few tries to get the hang of crocheting. Once you begin, you will find yourself eager and interested in taking on bigger and more challenging projects.

However, even the advanced projects are quite easy to master once you know the basics, so always have fun, and if you feel like you've hit a roadblock, don't worry-just look back on this book or patterns, and you'll be right back on track in no time. Good luck!

P.S.

Your opinion on the book you just read is very important to me!

My goal is to know how to publish books of better quality in the future and to update and improve existing ones.

So, it would be great to read your feedback.

Thank you

Regards,

Michelle Pfizer

Bonus

Printed in Great Britain
by Amazon

20197068R00068